For Gene,

Courage!

For future generations ~

Leigh + John

# WHAT UNITES US

# WHAT UNITES US

## Reflections on Patriotism

★ ★ ★

## DAN RATHER
### & Elliot Kirschner

ALGONQUIN BOOKS OF CHAPEL HILL
2017

Published by
ALGONQUIN BOOKS OF CHAPEL HILL
Post Office Box 2225
Chapel Hill, North Carolina 27515-2225

a division of
WORKMAN PUBLISHING
225 Varick Street
New York, New York 10014

Printed in the United States of America.
Published simultaneously in Canada by Thomas Allen & Son Limited.
Design by Anne C. Winslow.

Library of Congress Cataloging-in-Publication Data
Names: Rather, Dan, author. | Kirschner, Elliot, author.
Title: What unites us : reflections on patriotism /
Dan Rather & Elliot Kirschner.
Description: First edition. | Chapel Hill, North Carolina :
Algonquin Books of Chapel Hill, 2017. | Identifiers: LCCN 2017028401
(print) | LCCN 2017039612 (ebook) | ISBN 9781616207847 (ebook) |
ISBN 9781616207823 (hardcover : alk. paper) Subjects: LCSH:
Patriotism—United States. | National characteristics, American. |
Social values—United States. | LCGFT: Essays.
Classification: LCC JK1759 (ebook) | LCC JK1759.R35 2017 (print) |
DDC 323.6/5/0973—dc23
LC record available at https://lccn.loc.gov/2017028401

10 9 8 7 6 5 4 3 2 1
First Edition

To my grandsons, Martin and Andy, whose spirit
of service and love for this country fill me with pride
and confidence that our nation can unite and see
better days ahead.

—D. R.


To Malia, Eva, and Helena—my inspiration, hope,
and love.

—E. K.

"The greatness of America lies not in being more enlightened than any other nation, but rather in her ability to repair her faults."

—ALEXIS DE TOCQUEVILLE

# CONTENTS

# WHAT UNITES US

# Night Flights

The sun has set long ago and the sky is dark. I drive through a bustling metropolis, or a small town, or sometimes the lonely countryside. But there is one constant: My bags are packed and I am heading to an airport. I weave through busy city streets with neon signs. Buildings, too high to count the floors, stutter by me in the traffic. I head down rural roads—farms, fields, and forests flying by my window, illuminated only by my headlights and the infrequent passing car or truck.

Night flights have been a staple of my career heading to, from, and between datelines. Airports at night, especially when your flight is the last one out, are usually places of stillness. In the terminal, the shops and eateries are darkened and shuttered. Cleaning crews prepare for the coming day. I arrive at my gate and give a half nod to my fellow travelers. Most people understand that the expected behavior on a night flight is one of silence. This is a time when you are allowed, even encouraged, to be alone with your thoughts.

The taproot for this book was developed over my numerous journeys these many years. If I were to plot on a map my countless flight paths crisscrossing the United States, it would look like a thread stitching our great union together. Along the way, I have forged my own relationship with America, not only from the stories I have reported and the people I have met, but also during those many hours while I waited for sleep that only sometimes came. I look out the window at lights far below or, more often than not, just darkness. We are still a land of wide open spaces. As our great and diverse republic passes below me, I take a deep breath, close my eyes, and wonder: *Who are we? Where are we going?*

The opportunity for me and my generation to confront those questions is rapidly receding. Like the generations before us, we've risen to some challenges and shied away from others. We helped steer the United States through some perilous straits, but we find ourselves once again confronting rocky shoals. I worry about how important norms of American life are being shattered, along with a unity of purpose. I see the chasms of entrenched partisanship, growing inequality on income and opportunity, and the lingering injustices around race, gender, and sexual orientation. I think of my children and my grandchildren. How will they and their generations answer the call?

We hear often of America's destiny. All around Washington we see marble temples and monuments to our democracy. They look so solid and seem so rooted in history that we imagine them permanent features on the landscape. Never mind that those buildings, when compared to the life span of other nations, are but new construction. They were built to infuse a sense of awe and purpose in the populace of an improbable country. They are only as permanent as our ideals. And if we lose a sense of humility, we risk losing everything.

The true foundations for those buildings are not brick and stone, but our Constitution, our rule of law, our traditions, our work ethic, our empathy, our pragmatism, and our basic decency. As I have seen over the years, when we cultivate these instincts, we soar. When we sow seeds of division, hatred, and small-mindedness, we falter. As a wave of anxiety sweeps our nation, as big challenges loom before us, I feel an urgency.

America at its best is a wonderful, diverse, and spirited chorus. When we sing together, our message is amplified and it can shake the heavens. The songbook for our democracy is infused with our history, the joy of our glories and the pain of our failures. Its music and lyrics can and must be taught to those who will come after us.

This book is an effort to describe how that music sounds to me, to highlight the melodies that I find resonating in our republic's core strengths. I profess no great wisdom other than as a chronicler with the exceptional fortune of having had a front-row seat to much of our country's history. The issues I will raise are too big for any one voice to handle, and I hope my words will spark contemplation and discussion.

Over the years, I have been joined on these journeys by many treasured colleagues, and one of them is my friend and collaborator on this book, Elliot Kirschner. He and I are separated by many years, and we come from different backgrounds. But we share a deep love for the United States, its history, culture, and people. Our conversations over more than fifteen years of night flights, long car rides, meals, and drinks have helped hone our thoughts. This book is therefore a product of a unique partnership. Elliot's deep knowledge of the American journey and his gift for writing and storytelling have helped these essays immeasurably.

The United States does not belong to any one of us. Its strengths and riches give its citizens tremendous advantages, but we must not deplete them for the future. That wisdom and compassion can also extend beyond our borders. Many of my night flights have taken me around the globe, and I have seen that most people are rooting for the United States to succeed, not by virtue of its military or economic might, but because of our ideals.

As the cabin lights come on and the captain announces our final approach for landing, groggy passengers stir. A well-trained flight crew has delivered us safely to our destination. I see these air journeys as a metaphor for our national direction. We are bound together by our destiny, and we must work to ensure that there are calm and steady hands at the controls of our government. We can cover great distances, improbably escaping the limitations of gravity, if we choose to embrace the best of our traditions. This is what we hope to inspire with our book.

# What Is Patriotism?

When I was a young boy, we didn't have much in the way of material possessions. But around 1940 or '41, we got our first family car— a heavily used 1938 Oldsmobile that I can still see so clearly in my mind's eye. Its previous owner had lived along the Gulf of Mexico, and it was thus considered a "coastal car," which meant it was rusted, especially along the lower-left side. Its engine had also thrown a rod, blowing a big hole in the engine block, which had been patched. It was a bit of a rolling wreck, but I didn't see it as anything but beautiful.

In my neighborhood, the notion of a family vacation was an unheard-of luxury, something you might see in the movies but never expected to experience yourself. Yet that year, as the Fourth of July approached, my mother had the idea of driving to the beach in Galveston to see the fireworks over the Gulf of Mexico. My father was a little unsure of trusting the new car to take his young family on the round trip of roughly 100 miles, but my mother was persuasive. When the morning of the Fourth arrived, I was giddy with anticipation.

A trip from Houston to Galveston these days is relatively easy. At that time it was a big deal. There were no freeways, so we took the two-lane coastal road, and I remember how hot the day was. The humidity must have been approaching 100 percent. All the car windows were down, and to help the time pass, my mother had us sing patriotic songs. First and foremost was "America the Beautiful." She always thought it should have been made the national anthem, as it is less militaristic than "The Star-Spangled Banner" and easier to sing. I have inherited that opinion. We did sing "The Star-Spangled Banner" too, however, and there was a debate in the car about whether we should stop so that we could get out and stand while we were singing. We ultimately decided that we should probably keep going, our hands over our hearts as we sang. As proud Texans, we included several state songs in our repertoire ("Texas, Our Texas," "Beautiful Texas," and "The Yellow Rose of Texas"). I remember singing my heart out, and we repeated the songs over and over again, stopping to make sure my little brother and sister could learn the lyrics.

When we finally arrived in Galveston, it seemed magical. I can still taste the salt air and see the sun flickering on the rippling water of the Gulf. As we all sat on the seawall that had been built after the great hurricane of 1900, I thought this work of civil engineering was so marvelous it might as well have been the Great Wall of China. We played on the beach, and when the sun went down, we watched the fireworks. In retrospect, this was probably a modest show—low budget and low altitude—but I was transfixed. I had never seen anything like it. I oohed and aahed at the starlit night. I knew, after all, that "the stars at night are big and bright deep in the heart of Texas."

We had no money for the extravagances of a hotel, so the five of us slept in the car, curling up every which way. As we drove back the next morning, we were all a little stiff, but for that moment life seemed perfect. I have often wished I could have bottled that day to taste its sweet innocence once more. I had no way of knowing then that the country would soon be engulfed in war, and that some of the happy families we saw strolling the beach would have fathers go off to battle and never return. I didn't know that I soon would be stricken by rheumatic fever and confined to my bed. And I couldn't have anticipated that my parents, whom I can still picture sitting contentedly in the front seat, would pass away relatively early in my life. All I knew then was that I liked the feel of the road and the sight of the scenery going past. I liked going places . . . and I still do.

The open road has rightly become a symbol of America, a country whose destiny and people always seem to be on the move. And this family vacation helped fix an image of the United States in my mind as a land of wonder, awe, and optimism. Who can say definitely when and how it begins, that first, faint sense of place, of belonging; that trickle that eventually becomes a wellspring of deep emotional ties to one's homeland? Did it start when I entered grade school, with the every-morning ritual of saluting the flag, hand over heart? Did it begin by watching my father read the newspaper every day, worrying as the world moved toward war? Did it begin with the loving teachers who taught me about the special values of citizenship, values echoed by my parents at home? All I know is that every one of these experiences bound my developing world together in red-white-and-blue bunting.

Childhood is often sentimentalized, and I know now that the country I was growing to love had its flaws. I already knew the pain of the Great Depression and would soon live through the crisis of world war. I would then go on to a career that forced me to confront the often simmering and sometimes explosive injustices of the United States: its bigotry, exploitation, callousness, and corruption. It may seem counterintuitive, but these flaws made me love my country all the more.

For I have seen how a nation can pick itself up and make progress, even at divisive and dysfunctional political moments like the present when we seem to be spinning backward. I have found that the vast majority of men, women, and children I have met over the course of my life are kind and well intentioned. For all the stories of misdeeds on which I have reported, there have been many more of heroic actions and communal empathy, whether it is a public official resisting tremendous pressure and casting a vote of conscience or townspeople standing side by side to form a sandbag line against a raging river. It is true that the news headlines often paint a dark and dispiriting picture. But in every community, on every day, there are so many who choose to do the right thing.

Today we are a divided country. Too many decent and law-abiding men and especially women are being told that this nation is not for them, that their values make us weaker, that their voice is better left unspoken. We see elected officials pounding their chests, saying their vision of America represents the only real patriotism. To them I say that patriotism is not a cudgel. It is not an arms race. It also means confronting honestly what is wrong or sinful with our nation and government. I see my love of country imbued with a responsibility to bear witness to its faults.

Our nation was built on a foundation of ideals. To be sure, we are a country of natural wonder—a cross-continental expanse of fertile farmland, churning rivers, great resources, and some of the most beautiful places on Earth. But more than land, we are bound together by a grand experiment in government, the rule of law, and common bonds of citizenship. This is what it means to be an American. It's tragic that those with the strongest ancestral tie to the land, the Native Americans, have so bitterly felt the chasm between the soaring words of our Declaration of Independence and Constitution and the harsh reality of governmental policy. When tribes gathered to protest the oil pipeline at the Standing Rock Indian Reservation, the strength of the grievance was as much rooted in centuries of persecution as it was in the pipeline itself. Despite their inability to halt construction, those activists, facing at times violent suppression, reminded us that the right to peaceful protest, due process, and equal protection under the law should apply to all who live here.

Most Americans can trace their ancestors only as far as men and women who came to the United States well after its founding. But our creed has long been that all citizens can claim an equal legacy of this nation as their own, whether they just took the oath of citizenship or their family arrived on the *Mayflower*. We all are allowed to celebrate the Fourth of July as citizens, even though few of us have predecessors who were on this continent in 1776.

And we should neither forget nor be paralyzed by our prior national sins. We can all feel the swell of pride walking through our nation's capital city, even though we must tell the story of how some of those buildings were built by slave labor. We can revel in the opportunities of democracy, even though bigoted laws were passed in the chambers of Congress and upheld by the Supreme Court. We must look clear-eyed at the problems of the past and present, but be encouraged that our electoral and legal systems provide a framework for improved justice in the future.

In his 1963 "I Have a Dream" speech during the March on Washington, Dr. Martin Luther King Jr. offered one of the most eloquent personal visions of American patriotism ever delivered. Using the logic of economics to make a moral point, King called for an incredible debt to be paid. "In a sense we've come to our nation's capital to cash a check," he said. "When the architects of our republic wrote the magnificent words of the Constitution and the Declaration of Independence, they were signing a promissory note to which every American was to fall heir." The reckoning, King said, was long overdue: "We refuse to believe that the bank of justice is bankrupt. We refuse to believe that there are insufficient funds in the great vaults of opportunity of this nation. So we've come to cash this check, a check that will give us upon demand the riches of freedom and the security of justice."

In my mind, King wasn't calling for a revolution, even though that is how many at the time perceived it. He wasn't even arguing that there was something inherently rotten with the protections and provisions under which the United States was founded. Rather, he believed, and justly so, that the translation of those ideals into practice had been lacking. If our constitutional protections had been dispensed more equally and fairly, he asserted, then the dreams of which he spoke would be a lot closer to reality. King was not restrained in his criticism of the status quo, but he spoke freely and with the moral backing of our founding documents. In my years covering the civil rights movement, I was always struck by the fierce determination of these men and women to fight for their place in the future of a country that had mistreated them. They were infused with an unbreakable optimism that they would prevail. This spirit has been echoed time and again by those who have demanded their full constitutional rights as American citizens.

I have long been suspicious of those who would vociferously and publicly bestow the title of "patriot" upon themselves with an air of superiority. And I have generally taken a skeptical view of those who are quick to pass judgment on the depths of patriotism in others. George Washington, in his famous Farewell Address, warned future generations "to guard against the impostures of pretended patriotism." I like to think of this as an admonition, not only to be wary of the patriotic posturing of others, but also to be alert to the stirrings of pretended patriotism within oneself.

It is important not to confuse "patriotism" with "nationalism." As I define it, nationalism is a monologue in which you place your country in a position of moral and cultural supremacy over others. Patriotism, while deeply personal, is a dialogue with your fellow citizens, and a larger world, about not only what you love about your country but also how it can be improved. Unchecked nationalism leads to conflict and war. Unbridled patriotism can lead to the betterment of society. Patriotism is rooted in humility. Nationalism is rooted in arrogance.

The descent from patriotism to nationalism can be subtle and dangerous, and I am reminded of those weeks and months after the terror attacks of September 11, 2001. We had been grievously harmed, and it was only natural that we reacted by rallying together as Americans. But instead of asking ourselves hard questions about how we should proceed and making sure we did not forsake our democratic traditions, we wavered amid a climate of panic and hubris. In the name of protecting ourselves, we limited our civil liberties (the Patriot Act), undermined our moral traditions (torture), and ultimately launched a bloody and costly foreign misadventure (Iraq). Dissent, the rule of law, and deliberations on acts of war are all hallmarks of the best ideals of American patriotism, but they were marginalized during a fervor of nationalism.

A potent symbol of that era could be found in small pieces of metal that suddenly became ubiquitous. It is perhaps hard to remember, but whether or not a politician wore a flag pin became a big deal after 9/11, and for years thereafter. I see no reason not to wear a flag pin, if one is so inclined. But as President George W. Bush and his aides prominently displayed flag pins on their lapels, the subtext was clear. They were implying that their approach to the terror attacks was the patriotic one, an echo of the first rush of flag pin popularity during the Nixon administration, when the pins were sported by Republican politicians as a response to the antiwar and social protests.

In 2007, the then presidential candidate Barack Obama created a stir when he declined to wear a flag pin. He explained, "Shortly after 9/11, [the flag pin] became a substitute for, I think, true patriotism, which is speaking out on issues that are of importance to our national security."

In the end, however, the distraction became too great, and Obama returned to wearing a pin.

Patriotism—active, constructive patriotism—takes work. It takes knowledge, engagement with those who are different from you, and fairness in law and opportunity. It takes coming together for good causes. This is one of the things I cherish most about the United States: We are a nation not only of dreamers, but also of fixers. We have looked at our land and people, and said, time and time again, "This is not good enough; we can be better."

I have traveled many, many miles since that first family vacation. I have been blessed with a long and eventful life, where I have been able to see and learn so much. I have gone far beyond what I could have dreamed as a young boy. I know that I am a reporter who got lucky. I know that none of what I have been able to accomplish would have been possible without the great fortune of being born in the United States. I was taught by passionate teachers and have borne witness to men and women of far greater courage than I. There are so many who have sacrificed greatly, often with little recognition, to make this country a better, more just, and safer place to live.

Like so many, I love my country and its people. I do so with a sentimentality that may seem anachronistic in today's more jaded world. I have been known to get emotional when I talk about "the land of the free and the home of the brave." But to me these words mean something very deep, a feeling I struggle to put into words. They aren't just the lyrics before the umpire yells, "Play ball!" From battlefields to segregated lunch counters, I have seen the cost of freedom and bravery. It is high.

Our nation will not survive as we know it without an engaged and committed population. We cannot wait for others to fix what is broken, and I am inspired to see a new generation of grassroots activists rise up to insist that the cause of justice is expressed broadly across America. Our founding documents contain some of the most beautiful and noble words ever put on paper. I recite them often and love them with every fiber of my being. "We the people," all of us, are living together in perhaps the greatest social and governmental experiment ever conceived. We are being tested. How can we prepare ourselves for this moment? Are we up to the challenge?

# FREEDOM

★ ★ ★

# The Vote

I t would be nice to say that I came out of the womb with a deep sense of fairness, that I lectured my friends in the segregated schools of my youth about the injustice of institutional racism, that my family dinner table was a hotbed of passionate discussion about the evils of Jim Crow. I would like to be able to say all of that, but it would not be true. The truth is, for most of my early life I had too little consciousness about race, and I didn't have any deep personal empathy. It was just the way things were. It's not an excuse by any means. It was just a fact. The banality of racism and segregation was one of its most disturbing qualities.

There is one moment from my youth, however, that is seared in my mind (although I confess that my memory is likely not precise; it was a long time ago). The year was 1946,

I was in my early teens, and my father decided it was time I attend a precinct meeting to learn about civic life. The way politics in most states worked back then was that candidates were selected at state and national party conventions, not primaries. A precinct meeting chose delegates for a county convention, which selected delegates for the state or national party gatherings. So if you wanted a say in who your party nominee should be, you showed up at your precinct meeting. And in Texas in the 1940s, being a Democratic candidate was tantamount to election, just as it had been since the Civil War. My father once joked that if I wanted to see a Republican, he would take me to the Hermann Park zoo. He said they had a stuffed one there, and while he had heard there were great hordes of Republicans in the North, we hadn't seen a live one down in Texas for quite some time.

Precinct meetings were often raucous affairs, sort of like the old party conventions you see in historical documentaries—a far cry from the scripted events of today. Our gathering place was a ramshackle building that has since been rebuilt. And the man in charge was Papa Cosby, a longtime precinct chairman known for keeping the action moving. But that night, the first such event I had ever attended, was different. Even I could sense a hum in the air. I just didn't know the cause. It turned out that attendance at these meetings was normally an all-white and all-male affair of about maybe thirty-five to fifty people. But tonight there were four or five African American men also in attendance. By law they had every right to be there. It was their precinct too, as my neighborhood, the Heights, abutted a predominantly African American neighborhood. But law and custom can be very different things.

I remember grumblings, stares, and tension. The African American men made it clear that they were both citizens and veterans of the recent war. I seem to recall that they brought their service records with them. For a young man like me, it was exciting and yet unnerving. Without knowing that the evening would take this turn, my father had wanted me to be there. And yet I don't remember any slackening in his resolve to stay. Quite the contrary. Naively, I asked my father what was happening. He said that he would explain it all later, but he did nod toward the African American men and say, "When they get up, we get up." You voted in these meetings by standing. The precinct chair would say, "All those who support the measure, rise." So when a vote on a particular issue came up, and the African Americans rose, we rose as well. We stood up, the only white people to do so, and we were certainly noticed. I sensed the displeasure from others in the room. And I felt, as we walked out into the evening, some jostling in our path. Or maybe that was imagined.

I share this story not to suggest my father was a hero. For his time and place, he was remarkably unprejudiced. But he was not a trailblazer. His rationale in this case was straightforward: These men had fought in the war and they were entitled to vote. It wasn't a commitment to tear down all of Jim Crow. It was just a matter of fairness. I would like to say that this moment struck a deep moral chord within me that altered my trajectory on race from that moment forward. But it didn't fully register. I noted it and apparently filed it away for a time when I was more prepared to understand its lessons.

When I joined CBS News in 1962, I got myself assigned to the civil rights beat. It was emerging as an important national story, and again I would like to say I wanted to cover it because I sensed the moral import of the moment. But it was more that I saw it as a great opportunity for a reporter eager to be a witness to history, and to make a name for himself. One of my first stops was meeting Dr. Martin Luther King Jr. in Albany, Georgia. It was an early effort for his movement, and this one would ultimately end in failure. But being in the room with King, hearing him praise Mahatma Gandhi and nonviolent protest, sensing his deep spirituality based on both his Christian faith and his readings of philosophy—all of this started to focus me.

I then reported on a Ku Klux Klan rally, and then another one in rather short succession. Suddenly the stakes of the movement were very apparent. Seeing hate course through a crowd of hooded men and even some women as they rallied around a burning cross sent the chill of death down my spine. I remember trying to imagine what an African American would think, but in truth I couldn't really imagine. It is a level of hatred that is not easy to quench and that I fear still lives within too many. Today bigotry is often clothed in euphemism, and when I hear that kind of dog-whistle rhetoric, I remember those Klan rallies.

Armed with an appreciation of King's movement and the hatred that stood in his way, I headed to Jackson, Mississippi. As a reporter, I walked the streets, stepped into the cafés, and visited the churches to find out whom I should talk to, who mattered. I heard the obvious answers: The mayor. The local business leaders. And since it was the state capital, I sought out the legislators and others in government. But among the African Americans I met, particularly the pastors, one name kept coming up from the start: I needed to meet Mr. Evers. Medgar Evers.

By this point, Evers was in his late thirties and was already a veteran of the civil rights struggle, even if most of the country had not been paying close attention. Whereas

King sought a broad mandate of social change on a variety of issues—including, of course, the right to vote—Evers was different. He was focused like a laser beam on voting.

I remember meeting Evers for the first time, and if you were a fair judge of character, you couldn't help but be impressed. He would look you squarely in the eye when he spoke. But more than that, he was determined to bring your attention to the issue that occupied his entire being—the right to vote. Once again, I was slow to completely appreciate the importance of his particular cause, until I joined him one Election Day at a polling place on the outskirts of Jackson where African Americans were not allowed to vote. Evers and a group of black voters showed up with their papers. As they approached the white voting official at the door, some in the group seemed to tremble, understandably. Not Evers. I learned later that he had done this many times before.

What proceeded was a simple morality play, but one that shaped me as much or more than almost any other event in my lifetime. The voting official said, "What you doing here, boy?" And Evers politely responded that he had come with these fine people to vote. "You aren't voting today, you aren't voting any day," came the reply. The words on the page cannot do any justice to the terror and violence in the voice. Evers explained that they had all their papers and were registered, knowing full well the response. "Well, I'm telling you," the official answered, "they ain't gonna vote."

Suddenly everything snapped to attention in my mind. I remembered going to the polling places with my father as early as I could walk, and the great pride with which he filled out his ballot—my father, whom at this point in 1962 I had just buried weeks earlier after his death in an automobile accident. I remembered the faces of the African American men at the precinct meeting, and standing when they stood. I retroactively understood the deep sin of segregation and racism that had enveloped me my entire life.

To write this now is to be shocked anew by my naïveté and blindness. I wish I had seen all of this earlier. But the brazenness of a white election official tossing aside the constitutional right of enfranchisement, a right that entered the Constitution only after the Civil War, our bloodiest conflict, made me seethe with anger. I was standing off to the side, watching this transpire. I don't remember having a camera crew at the time. Those days we often traveled without one, as showing up with a camera was considered a provocative act by local officials. But I do remember sharing my experience later with my soundman, who was from Alabama.

"What did you expect to happen?" he asked.

"Not that," I said.

"Well, that's how it is in a lot of places," he said.

There was a disconnect back then between what was happening in the South and what the rest of the nation knew. Many people had no idea these kinds of things were taking place. Even some of my bosses back at CBS News headquarters in New York wondered how widespread and entrenched these types of actions were. Did this happen all the time, or was it a rare occurrence? Was it being staged? I knew what I was seeing and I was determined to bring this story into living rooms across the nation. This was not America as I had envisioned it. And I wanted my countrymen and women to know this too. I felt a great certainty in the separation of right from wrong. My relationship with my country would never be the same. Patriotism would require standing up to what I had seen, not standing alongside it in silence.

I witnessed in Medgar Evers that day the very definition of courage and love of country—his country, my country, our country. After that moment, Evers and I spent more time together. We got to be a bit more than acquaintances, and we often shared a cola and a conversation in the shank of the evening after I had finished filing for the late radio news. Remarkably, I found very little hatred in the man. He didn't hate white people, although I felt he had every right to. He hated the system and the elected officials who manipulated it. But he saw most of his white neighbors as decent

Christian people who were just horribly misguided on race. They had grown up in a system they never questioned and never really understood.

However, I had a sense from that first reporting trip that Evers was living on borrowed time. To stand up for the right to vote was to challenge all the power of the Southern status quo.

I was in Tuscaloosa, Alabama, in June of 1963 when we got the call, and it came from King's headquarters. Evers had been shot and killed. My crew and I chartered a plane, getting to Jackson before daybreak and any other national reporters. Evers had been shot on his front porch, while his wife and children were at home, by a coward hiding in the grass across the street. It was a calculated and cold-blooded assassination. The murder scene was eerily quiet. There were some local law enforcement, and eventually other reporters showed up, but I don't remember any large crowds.

As I reported from the city, I found that African Americans' feelings ranged from outrage to despondency. This was what happened when someone tried to stand up and lead. But there was also a deep resolve to persist. Among white people, there were certainly a fair number who felt that Evers had gotten what he deserved. The majority just wanted to go about their lives as if nothing had happened. There might have been white people in Jackson who would have told me this was terrible, that we needed to get to the bottom of it, that we needed to change our ways. But if those people were there, I didn't find them.

Myrlie Evers would tell me later how terrified she was. She wasn't only in shock and mourning the sudden death of her husband; she was frightened about what might happen to her children. I wish all those who so glibly try to suppress the vote today could be forced to look into her eyes as I did that day in Jackson.

So many of our problems today are directly linked to the way we vote or how we are subtly prohibited from voting. In some ways, we have worked hard to enhance the ease of casting a ballot; we have early voting and voting by mail in many states. On the other hand, there are states seeking to limit access to the ballot box, even if they make claims to the contrary. And often these voter suppression efforts target the most marginal members of society. We see long lines at some precincts and short lines at others. It is easier for a white-collar worker to alter his or her schedule to vote, but for a single mother punching a clock with a long bus ride to her job, limiting voting options can amount to disenfranchisement.

It is one of the great truisms of a democratic form of government that not only political power but the very definition of citizenship is predicated on the right to vote. The

Voting Rights Act of 1965 did much to fulfill the widespread enfranchisement for African Americans promised in 1870 in the Fifteenth Amendment. But a recent Supreme Court ruling has removed key provisions of the Voting Rights Act, and many of the gains we've seen are being curtailed under specious claims of voter fraud. So we see states passing voter ID laws and other hurdles, even though the truth is that in-person voter fraud is so rare as to be statistically nonexistent. The real danger to the sanctity of the vote lies in suppression.

It is inevitable that the battle lines of the recent voting wars have centered on race. Indeed, these narratives—race and voting—are inextricably intertwined. Full citizenship has been an elusive goal for many African Americans, long after the bondage of slavery was lifted. (And for African American women, as for all women, it would require an additional amendment to the Constitution to get the right to vote.) Those who seek to suppress voting today are either ignorant of the history or are, as I suspect is more often the case, malevolently choosing to ignore it. I am loath to judge the hearts of others on this matter, because I too was naive. Perhaps part of the problem is that schools don't teach enough of what happened then and is still happening now.

To suppress the vote is to make a mockery of democracy. And those who do so are essentially acknowledging that their policies are unpopular. If you can't convince a majority of voters that your ideas are worthy, you try to limit the pool of voters. This reveals a certain irony: Many who are most vocal in championing a free, open, and dynamic economy are the same political factions that suppress these principles when it comes to the currency of ideas. I think the record is clear that our republic has benefited from the expansion of suffrage.

We see disenfranchisement occurring not only with how people are allowed to vote, but also for whom. Gerrymandering isn't just a recent phenomenon, though; the word was coined in 1812 when Massachusetts governor Elbridge Gerry went to such egregious lengths to redraw the state senate districts in his party's favor that one district took on the shape of a salamander. More recently, gerrymandering has been taken to a new extreme, and neither of the major political parties is entirely blameless. Aided by powerful computer data analysis, it is now possible to draw district lines in such a way as to swing considerably the balance of state legislative and congressional delegations. Gerrymandering is now often used to stifle minority representation by congregating voters in districts to lessen their overall political power, and some of the fiercest court battles on voting are taking place in this arena.

Even beyond the legal hurdles to voting, a shrinking

and polarized electorate damages our democracy. We need elected officials who represent wide swaths of the population, not narrow gerrymandered silos. Our republic relies on a marketplace of ideas, but creating safe seats for both Republicans and Democrats removes the very competition for votes that is at the heart of our democracy. It lessens enthusiasm and civic engagement, which leads to apathy. One can actively suppress votes or make voting seem meaningless. They are two paths to the same destination. Our voting participation is far below the levels of a healthy democracy, and this should worry all of us who care about the United States. We need to be creative in finding new ways to get more people to vote. Instead we seem to be going backward.

In that neighborhood precinct meeting many decades ago, I saw democracy as an activity and a civic duty. I saw the same thing in the determination of Medgar Evers and his followers. Of course, casting a ballot is just one of our civic duties, but a vital one. It is an act of speech, a demand that your voice be heard, that you are included in the republic. Lessening this bond of citizenship, either forcibly or through indifference, makes us less free and less resilient as a nation. I hope we can continue and regain our footing on a path of greater enfranchisement. The coherence of our national destiny depends on it.

# Dissent

I t takes a special brand of courage to forge a path against a marching crowd. We may live in a democracy of majority rule, but one of our most important founding ideals was to confer legal protection on those unafraid to buck popular sentiment with contrarian voices. Dissent can sometimes be uncomfortable, but it is vital in a democracy. Our nation would never have thrived without the determination of those who were fearless in their beliefs, even when those beliefs were severely out of step with the popular mood and those in power. And in moments like the present, when our government has become erratic and threatens our constitutional principles, dissent is doubly necessary to resist a slide into greater autocracy.

I grew up in a segregated and bigoted world in dire

need of dissenting voices. My parents, teachers, friends, and acquaintances mostly accepted the status quo without question, and I have come to learn that most people, in most times, tend to follow the herd. That is why our First Amendment is so important. Free speech must be protected so that we can hear from those who challenge our beliefs. And a free and independent press is essential for bringing dissenting opinions to the national conversation.

My first inklings of the importance of dissent came during the anti-communist witch hunts of the early 1950s, epitomized by the reign of terror under Wisconsin senator Joseph McCarthy. But Houston and East Texas had already been a hotbed for such activity; before McCarthy, there was Martin Dies Jr., a local congressman who chaired the House Un-American Activities Committee before and during World War II. He was a classic demagogue who railed against a federal government riddled with "hundreds of left-wingers and radicals who do not believe in our system of private enterprise." It was a tragic preamble to the much larger destruction to come.

When the anti-communist fervor reached its apex in the United States in the decade after the war, the crackdown hit Houston particularly hard, as documented in Don Carleton's book *Red Scare*. The city had a very active chapter of the Minute Women of the U.S.A., a national group of middle- and upper-class women dedicated to ferreting out supposed "un-Americans" in government and education. And it was in the schools where the most significant battle lines in town were drawn. In 1952, the Minute Women and other like-minded groups put forward a slate of ardent anti-communists for the school board, setting up a showdown with moderates on the ballot. It was one of the biggest local news stories of the year.

In the end, some candidates from each group were elected, which suggests that there were many in Houston who refused to be swept up in the mania. But the Minute Women, working in close association with many of the city's male power structure, did wreak tremendous damage on individual lives. They forced out teachers and administrators who they felt were communists, as well as those they deemed not fervent enough in their anti-communism. Their biggest success was the takedown of the deputy superintendent, Dr. George Ebey, on trumped-up charges of being a communist sympathizer—a development of such significance it was covered by *Time* magazine.

After college and a short stint in the Marines, I got a brief tryout to work at the *Houston Chronicle* in 1954 under the editorship of Martin Emmet Walter, a strident anti-communist. Walter had a merciless eye—and fierce tongue—for any reporter who even subtly deviated from his strict conservative orthodoxy. The *Chronicle*'s editorial page was a soapbox for some of the vilest propaganda of the day.

I didn't last long at the newspaper (too poor at spelling, for one thing), but the *Chronicle* moved me over to the radio station the paper owned, and we started doing daily reports from the city desk in the paper's newsroom. It was there that I got a wonderful mentor in an editor named Dan Cobb, the first dissenter I ever got to know. He understood well, and would verbalize, the dangers of the age. He had no tolerance for the malignancy of the Red Scare, but he also knew that Walter, as editor, could hold the newsroom in a perpetual state of panic. Every day I would watch Cobb make the rounds of the reporter desks with the demeanor of a village priest or rabbi. He would provide quiet but encouraging counsel. "I know you are worried, but we have to outlast this," he would say in hushed tones. "We must work within the confines of the possible; it is our job to report the news as straight as we can."

One evening I was reporting live on the radio from the newspaper's city desk on a round of contentious school board elections when some results came in that were bad for a slate of anti-communist candidates on the ballot. I made some mention of it on the air, not knowing that Walter was behind me. He grabbed my microphone and yelled into it, "This young man doesn't know what he's talking about."

He stormed off, leaving me shaken and distraught. Cobb came over immediately to steady my young nerves, reminding me that as a reporter it was my job to tell it as I saw it.

There were many reporters at the *Chronicle* who were horrified by the editorial direction the paper had taken, and they each had a decision to make: Should they quit in defiance, or try to stay and do the best they could? Cobb knew that if he pushed too far, he and his reporters would likely be fired and replaced by those not afraid to toe the company line. It is that age-old dilemma: Do you stay and try to change the church from within, or leave the church? Cobb and the others decided to stay and push back in subtle ways. Oftentimes Walter would want a straight news story rewritten to give it his preferred slant, but Cobb would go ahead and publish the original, claiming he was on deadline and couldn't incorporate the new copy. It was a subtle form of dissent, but it was effective.

The drama playing out at the *Chronicle* paled in comparison to the dangers posed to the nation at large. Over the course of just a few years, thousands of lives were broken by lost jobs and shattered reputations. Some of the victims were famous, like those on the Hollywood Blacklist. Most, however, were everyday people: teachers, public officials, and those working in the private sector. It is now widely understood that it was the persecutors who were "un-American," not the persecuted. But too much of the country had looked the other way until the fever broke.

One of the lessons of the Red Scare is that the long arc of history often validates the dissenters, and a particularly striking example of this is the Vietnam War. Today it is largely acknowledged to have been a tragic mistake, but when I first went to cover the war in 1965–66, the conflict and the anti-communist impulses that fueled it were still largely popular across the political spectrum, but especially with politicians in Washington. The Pentagon was painting a rosy picture of the state of the conflict, but by the mid-1960s the folly of Vietnam was apparent to many of the young men who were ordered to fight and die in that distant jungle hell. And those of us who went out to cover the combat saw it too.

There were some dissenting voices on Vietnam from the beginning, but they tended to be on the far end of the political left. Mark Hatfield, a moderate Republican governor from Oregon, was a notable exception. In 1966, he was the only governor to vote "no" on support of the war at the annual conference of governors, and in the fall of that year, Hatfield rode his antiwar stance to the Senate. He defeated the pro-war incumbent, Democrat Robert Duncan, who had dramatically claimed that the stakes were "whether Americans will die in the buffalo grass of Vietnam or the rye grass of Oregon." With backing from the voters of Oregon, Hatfield turned dissent into political victory. That is how our system of democracy is supposed to work.

Another dissenter of note was Minnesota senator Eugene McCarthy, who broke with President Lyndon Johnson, a fellow Democrat, over the war. McCarthy was a source of mine in Washington—not a secret source, but a good one. He was iconoclastic and scholarly—not your typical senator. I knew that McCarthy's dread about Vietnam weighed heavily on him, but I was still surprised when he announced that he would challenge President Johnson for the 1968 Democratic nomination. "I am concerned that the administration seems to have set no limit to the price which it is willing to pay for a military victory," he explained. McCarthy became a pariah in his own party, and few felt his quixotic candidacy would have much effect.

After the North Vietnamese and the Vietcong launched the Tet Offensive in January of 1968, popular opinion further shifted against the war. This was especially true among the Democratic electorate, and McCarthy's candidacy galvanized the antiwar vote. When McCarthy came close to defeating Johnson in the New Hampshire primary, New York senator Bobby Kennedy jumped into the race, and President Johnson announced: "I shall not seek, and I will not accept, the nomination of my party for another term as your president." McCarthy's dissent had helped shape the course of history.

With what we now know about Vietnam, it may be tempting to retroactively portray the war critics as travelers on a path of inevitability. But that was not how it felt back then. Dissent is most controversial during wartime because it is cast as unpatriotic and dangerous to the national cause. But that is precisely the time when a democracy should be asking itself difficult and uncomfortable questions.

In January 1968, five thousand antiwar protesters—mostly women—gathered in Washington under the banner of the Jeannette Rankin Brigade in honor of the eighty-seven-year-old woman walking proudly in the front row of the procession. Rankin, a fierce critic of the Vietnam War, had a long history of political activism. In 1916, she had become the first woman ever elected to Congress, a Republican representative from Montana, confidently stating, "I may be the first woman member of Congress, but I won't be the last."

Rankin was an avowed pacifist, and in 1917, she was one of only fifty representatives (and six senators) to vote against American entry into World War I. "I felt . . . the first time the first woman had a chance to say no to war, she should say it," she explained. Rankin served one term, losing a race for Senate in 1918. But she was reelected to the

House in 1940, just in time for another fateful vote. When the Japanese attacked Pearl Harbor on December 7, 1941, Rankin followed her pacifist conscience again and cast the sole vote against declaring war. "As a woman," she said, "I can't go to war, and I refuse to send anyone else." This act of dissent was so unpopular that it ended her political career. I disagree strongly with Rankin's vote on war with Japan. But I also feel that we are a better and stronger nation for having such voices. The role of dissent is to force all of us to question our dogmas and biases. It is to stretch the spectrum of discourse.

In the same vein, on April 4, 1967, Dr. Martin Luther King Jr. took the pulpit at Riverside Church in New York for one of the most consequential and controversial speeches of his career. It was entitled "Beyond Vietnam: A Time to Break Silence," and most Americans weren't ready for the message he would deliver. Instead of the optimism of "I Have a Dream," there was a weariness verging on pessimism. "The war in Vietnam is but a symptom of a far deeper malady within the American spirit," King said. ". . . We as a nation must undergo a radical revolution of values." King preached about money going for bombs instead of to the needy, about the uneven burden of military service between the rich and the poor, and about the institutionalization of violence at the heart of all wars. King described the plight of the Vietcong and argued that the world would see us as occupiers. In perhaps his most controversial statement, he equated the use of napalm by the U.S. military with the tactics of Nazi Germany. "What do they think as we test out our latest weapons on them, just as the Germans tested out new medicine and new tortures in the concentration camps of Europe?"

I was not in the pews that evening, but I remember reading the press coverage and feeling a deep ache in my heart. The thought occurred that perhaps King had gone too far. He might have gotten a standing ovation from his antiwar audience, but the larger response to the speech was highly negative. The *New York Times* ran an editorial entitled "Dr. King's Error" that suggested, in an observation echoed by many commentators and even some of King's allies, that the civil rights leader should have kept his focus on racial justice instead of war.

But King saw these causes as inextricably linked. A few days after the speech, he was captured on an FBI surveillance tape in a heated debate with his friend Stanley Levison. Levison worried the speech was a disaster that played into the hands of their critics. King was resolute in response. "I figure I was politically unwise but morally wise. I think I have a role to play which may be unpopular." That quote is as elegant a definition of dissent as you are likely to find.

In all the sanitized reimaginings of King's legacy, the Riverside Church speech is too often forgotten. That is a mistake because it captures both the complexities of the times and of a man who was one of the great dissenters in American history. King had exhorted his audience "to move beyond the prophesying of smooth patriotism" to "a firm dissent based upon the mandates of conscience and the reading of history." I like the phrases "smooth patriotism" and "firm dissent" because fighting for justice is rarely smooth and dissent requires steely resolve.

What is perhaps most striking about the Riverside Church speech, and something I think too often misunderstood about King, is his strong belief that communism was not the answer. For while he was highly critical of the United States, he told his audience, "We must not engage in a negative anti-communism, but rather in a positive thrust for democracy, realizing that our greatest defense against communism is to take offensive action in behalf of justice." One of the more remarkable interchanges I had in an interview with Fidel Castro was when the Cuban communist firebrand expressed his complete bafflement as to why King and other civil rights leaders in the United States had not embraced communism, as so many other protest and revolutionary groups around the world had. I think the answer lies in the nature of principled dissent. We have a long history in the United States of marginalized voices eventually convincing majorities through the strength of their ideas. Our democratic machinery provides fertile soil where seeds of change can grow. Few knew that better than King.

While some dissenters are famous, most act on much smaller stages. But that does not mean their actions are any less courageous. To stand up and say something isn't right takes guts, no matter who you are, but it is especially true for those who have traditionally been more vulnerable members of society. Recently, there has been a growing awareness of harassment in the workplace, particularly the kind inflicted by powerful men on less powerful women. As a young reporter, I knew of famous senators who were "girdle snappers" on the congressional elevators, and while such brazen behavior wouldn't be tolerated today, we still see how companies, organizations, universities, the military, and others too often have looked the other way on actions that aren't only repulsive but also illegal. Whatever progress we have made is because many brave women, and some brave men, have stepped forward with stories that they insisted the rest of us hear.

Dissenters are not always right. They are certainly not all people one would admire, and sometimes their motives are complicated or unknowable. Do we consider Edward Snowden, the former CIA employee who leaked sensitive secrets about surveillance programs from the U.S. government, to be a dissenter? Some see him as a hero and others see him as a traitor. His reasons for his actions remain opaque, despite his multiple public statements. I find it difficult to understand why he assumed that he single-handedly had enough wisdom to decide to release highly sensitive government secrets, but you cannot deny the effect he had. American policy has changed profoundly. I do not know how history will judge Snowden, but it is a good reminder of how dissent can look up close and in real time. It is messy. It is controversial. But it often is consequential.

The United States was born from perhaps one of the most radical lines of dissenting speech in human history, the idea that the citizens of a land should live by the consent of the governed and not the whims of a monarch. Republican president Dwight D. Eisenhower famously paid homage to this history in a 1954 speech during the height of the Red Scare: "Here in America we are descended in blood and in spirit from revolutionaries and rebels—men and women who dared to dissent from accepted doctrine. As their heirs, may we never confuse honest dissent with disloyal subversion." Unfortunately, we have seen in our history too many cases where "honest dissent" was confused with "disloyal subversion," but one place where dissent is actively fostered is in the law. This is especially true at the Supreme Court, where many of the most famous dissents have pointed the way for the future direction of the country.

Back in 1896 in *Plessy v. Ferguson*, all but one justice voted to uphold legalized segregation and the so-called separate but equal doctrine. The lone dissenter was Justice John Marshall Harlan, who famously admonished his fellow jurists and the nation as a whole: "Our Constitution is color-blind, and neither knows nor tolerates classes among citizens. In respect of civil rights, all citizens are equal before the law. The humblest is the peer of the most powerful." More than a half century later, the Supreme Court would validate Harlan's humanity with a unanimous decision in *Brown v. Board of Education*. Over the decades, dissents on the court have also pointed the way forward on the right to privacy, criminal justice reforms, gay rights, and other protections on which the law has moved toward what were once minority views.

In World War I, the country was gripped with a paranoia not unlike that found during the Red Scare. Congress passed an Espionage Act and a Sedition Act that were used to prosecute and imprison men and women for their speech, including the famous socialist labor leader Eugene Debs, who would run for president in 1920 while in prison and garner nearly one million votes. These restrictions on dissent were brought to the Supreme Court, and they were resoundingly upheld. And yet out of this period of restriction came one of the most stirring articulations of the importance of dissent in American history. Fittingly, and perhaps almost poetically, it came in an actual dissent.

The case was *Abrams v. United States* (1919), and it involved a group of Russian immigrants who had distributed pamphlets advocating against the war effort. They were arrested under laws limiting speech and were sentenced to up to twenty years in prison. The Supreme Court justices had twice ruled unanimously to uphold the constitutionality of congressional acts to stifle dissent during World War I, and in both cases, the opinion was written by Justice Oliver Wendell Holmes. But in the wake of the previous decisions, Holmes had been beset by friends and legal scholars who felt he and the court had gone too far in suppressing speech. When the decision came down in *Abrams*, the convictions were upheld, but it was not unanimous. Two justices dissented, including Holmes.

Holmes was one of the greatest legal minds in American history, and what emerged from his dissent in *Abrams* is a passionate plea for the importance of dissent and free expression. Holmes had come to his decision by listening to others who had disagreed with him. His dissent was, therefore, a product of dissent. He had been challenged in a marketplace of ideas, and he had changed his mind. Now he was determined that others have the same opportunity.

"The ultimate good desired is better reached by free trade in ideas . . . ," Holmes wrote in his dissent. "The best test of truth is the power of the thought to get itself accepted in the competition of the market, and that truth is the only ground upon which their wishes safely can be carried out. That, at any rate, is the theory of our Constitution. . . . I think that we should be eternally vigilant against attempts to check the expression of opinions that we loathe and believe to be fraught with death, unless they so imminently threaten immediate interference with the lawful and pressing purposes of the law that an immediate check is required to save the country."

The strength of Justice Holmes's dissent shaped the future of American law. How we conceive of our First Amendment protections today much more closely resembles his views than that of the majority in *Abrams*. And yet, the need to remain vigilant in protecting the right to dissent remains as urgent as ever. Recently we have seen a level of public protest unlike anything we have witnessed in decades. Dissent is about marching, and making one's voice heard in the streets and at the ballot box. But at the same time, there are strong voices calling this dissent unpatriotic and dangerous. We cannot let the forces of suppression win. America works best when new thoughts can emerge to compete, and thrive, in a marketplace of ideas. It's a testimony to the wisdom of those who founded our republic and to the courage of all the dissenters who have come forward ever since.

# The Press

In his novel *1984*, George Orwell laid out a dystopian vision of a world where words cease to have meaning, history is continually rewritten, and the notion of truth is forever lost. The book was first published in 1949 (in the aftermath of World War II and the dawn of the Cold War), but its exploration of a society in which propaganda is the only currency of communication is resonant once more. I am not surprised that a new generation of readers is seeking out Orwell's masterpiece to make sense of our current age.

Orwell understood that a government that is beyond the reach of accountability has little incentive to tell the truth. Indeed, its power may arise from the obliteration of objective facts. In the world of *1984*, contradictory statements lose all sense of context and we are left with preposterous slogans: "War Is Peace. Freedom Is Slavery. Ignorance Is Strength." And yet Orwell asks us, if there is no one with the power to call out a lie as a lie, does it end up ceasing to be a lie?

Orwell certainly was not the first to perceive the corrupting effects of unfettered power on the discourse of democracy. Our Founding Fathers, after breaking free from monarchical subjugation, were determined to construct a government of checks and balances on absolute concentrated power. So they created a federal system with differentiations between state and national control, as well as three branches of government with distinct powers and responsibilities that had to answer to one another. But, not satisfied that that was enough, they added ten amendments to the Constitution. And in the very first of those amendments, they established what has become an insurance policy for the continued health of the republic: a free press. As a working journalist, I know I have a stake in this concept. But as a grandfather who wants to see his grandchildren live in a country at least as free as the one I have enjoyed, a free press is even more relevant now than ever.

The role of the press is to ask hard questions and refuse to be deterred even when someone powerful claims, "Nothing to see here." At first glance, it might seem as if the press is a destabilizing force: It can undermine the credibility of our elected officials and ultimately our confidence in government. It can drive down stock prices and embolden our nation's critics and enemies. It can uncover inconvenient truths and stir divisions within our society. But our Founders understood that long-term accountability is more important than short-term stability. Where would America be without the muckrakers of the progressive era, like Ida Tarbell, who uncovered the perfidy and immorality of the Standard Oil monopoly under John D. Rockefeller; without the *New York Times*'s publishing of the Pentagon Papers, which exposed the lies around the Vietnam War; without the dogged work of the *Boston Globe* in documenting sexual abuse within the Catholic Church? Because of the press, powerful institutions were held accountable for their actions, and we became a stronger nation.

Presently, the institution of a free press in America is in a state of crisis greater than I have ever seen in my lifetime, and perhaps in any moment in this nation's history. The winds of instability howl from many directions: a sustained attack on press freedom from those in political power, crumbling business models, rapidly changing technologies, and some self-inflicted wounds. This is a test, not only for those of us who work in journalism, but also for the nation as a whole.

The most immediate threat comes from the dangerous

political moment in which we find ourselves. We have seen individual journalists and some of our best press institutions singled out for attack by the highest of elected officials for reporting truths that the powerful would rather remain hidden; for pointing out lies as lies; and for questioning motivations that deserve scrutiny. It would be easy to fill this essay, and indeed entire volumes, with examples of these recent outrages against the press and to call out the chief culprits in these assaults on our constitutional freedoms. I suspect much scholarship in the future will be dedicated to just such topics. But I am less interested in naming names than in explaining the larger forces at play, which have been years, if not decades, in the making.

Of course there has always been friction between those in power and the journalists tasked with covering them. George Washington complained that the press treated him unfairly, and I imagine every president since then has felt similarly at some point in his tenure in office. But as a public official in the United States, you agree to subject yourself and your actions to scrutiny. And for most of my early life and career, I had a sense that politicians, especially those at the national level, understood this compact. Even as they tried to hide things or shift attention away from scandal, they knew they could not afford to disengage from the press.

The presidency of Richard Nixon was different and

became an inflection point in the history of the free press in the United States. That he was ultimately brought down by investigative journalism does not diminish the damage done during his tenure in office. In the decades since, we have learned of the lengths he was secretly willing to go to to undermine the press, such as tapping into reporters' phone lines and pressuring their corporate bosses. But even Nixon's public statements, as well as his public actions, made clear his antipathy to the fourth estate; he attacked the press, disengaged from them, and instituted a strategy of sidelining national media outlets in favor of staged events and interviews with local reporters—reporters who, in what would likely be their one and only interview with a president, were less willing to ask hard questions.

The ignominy with which Nixon left office should not detract from the effectiveness of his press strategy. And it is not an accident that one of the architects of this strategy was a young Roger Ailes, who would advise future Republican presidents and then monetize the demonization of a supposedly "biased" press by creating Fox News. Ailes understood that there were long-simmering currents among millions of Americans who felt persecuted by liberal elites and by extension the national press headquartered in places like New York. This antagonism was not theoretical and could be violent. Senator Joseph McCarthy tarred journalists during the communist witch hunts (during which time CBS was called the "Communist Broadcasting System"), and later local and state politicians attacked the press for its coverage of civil rights (and CBS gained the nickname the "Colored Broadcasting System"). But Nixon was the first to do it on the national level—and win the presidency. I don't think those of us in the press grasped the full import of what had happened.

None of us could have predicted how technological and regulatory changes would usher in a new media landscape that, building on the Nixon legacy, would transform the very nature of news. In 1987, under President Ronald Reagan, the Federal Communications Commission (FCC) abolished the Fairness Doctrine. In place since 1949, it had stipulated equal airtime for differing points of view. In this environment where media outlets felt less compelled to present balanced political debate, AM radio stations in particular started to switch to a lucrative form of programming best exemplified by Rush Limbaugh—right-wing talk radio. For hours on end, Limbaugh, and others who followed his lead, would present their view of the world without rebuttal, fact-checking, or any of the other standards in place at most journalistic outlets. Often their commentary included bashing any media coverage that conflicted with the talk-radio narrative.

In the 1980s and 1990s the advent of cable television

broadened what had been a limited number of stations into a diverse lineup of niche networks. Into this business opportunity stepped Fox News and Mr. Ailes. The sales pitch here was subtler than talk radio; Fox News portrayed itself as a full-fledged news outlet that was a corrective to the liberal press. There are some fine journalists who have worked and continue to work at Fox News. But the majority of programming is opinion rather than news, and this opinion is often in service of conservative political objectives regardless of the facts.

More recently, the entire journalism business model has been upended by the rise of the Internet and, even more recently, social media. Suddenly anyone can be a news publisher, regardless of their expertise, sense of fairness, or motives. In this digital free-for-all, the *New York Times* can seem like just another website alongside a propaganda outfit like Breitbart. And "fake news" from individual or state actors can spread like wildfire through Facebook, Twitter, and other similar outlets. In *1984*, Orwell could only imagine a tyrannical central government having the power to systematically undermine objective truth. Today we see that process happening organically through millions of social media "shares."

I know my critics will claim the narrative I have laid out above is proof of my own liberal bias. It is a charge I have heard for decades, a personal echo of the larger attacks on this nation's major journalistic institutions. I do not think the bias attack against the American press holds up to scrutiny. Reporters by their nature tend to be suspicious, especially of accrued power, and that usually extends to party politics. Democratic presidents have had to withstand withering press coverage, from Lyndon Johnson's handling of the Vietnam War to Jimmy Carter's reputation for ineffectualness. And with some of this coverage, like the overblown Whitewater "scandal" during Bill Clinton's term and the distortions around Barack Obama's health care bill, Democrats have argued that they have been treated unfairly by the press—with some justification. I have no doubt that many conservatives believe that the press is biased, but I believe the political leaders and activists who assiduously stoke these fears are doing so cynically. They see press attacks as a way to rally their base and distract voters from the weaknesses of their own candidates, without having to answer specific allegations.

The effects of the sustained attacks on the press have become cumulative, intimidating reporters—and, more important, editors, publishers, and owners—in newsrooms across the country. Despite the negative perception in some circles, almost every American journalist I have ever met is at the core patriotic. We wish our fellow Americans well.

We hope our government leads with moral clarity and wisdom. And we want it to succeed in making us a more peaceful, prosperous, and just country. Nevertheless, our constitutional role often puts us in an adversarial position to our government. These days, I fear that the pull of our inborn patriotism combined with a fear of being labeled un-American clouds that role, with real and potentially corrosive effect. These are forces every journalist must be aware of, and on guard against. But often our individual defenses fail, and sometimes they fail en masse with disastrous consequences. I consider my biggest journalistic failure to be one in which I unfortunately was not alone. In the lead-up to the second Iraq War, when the American public needed a strong and independent press, too many of us blinked and the nation was far worse for our drifting from our core purpose.

On the morning of September 11, 2001, as I rushed to the CBS News broadcast studio, I could see the columns of smoke rising amid a brilliant blue sky. I knew that our country was facing a bloody and tragic test, the depths of which would be unknowable for some time. It is easy to forget what those days, weeks, and months that followed felt like. "Al-Qaeda" became a household word, and there was palpable fear that another large-scale attack was imminent. The immediate task in newsrooms like ours was to make sense of the moment. Reporters worked long, difficult shifts chasing down the names of the victims and telling the stories of the families they left behind. We investigated how the horrific terrorist plan had come together, and how it was executed. We provided context by examining al-Qaeda attacks of the past, and we explained the rise of Osama bin Laden. The American public was contending with waves of sorrow, pain, fear, and anger. They were hungry to know more about what had happened.

The focus shifted almost immediately to Afghanistan, where the masterminds of the mass murder of 9/11 had found sanctuary. And when American men and women in uniform headed to Afghanistan to fight, reporters were embedded with units to cover the story. In general, there was not enough skepticism at the time in our reporting. We should have asked harder questions about whether we were committing enough resources to the war, and whether the special operations–led campaign was the right approach.

Then, almost immediately, we started hearing from high-level officials in the George W. Bush administration, especially Vice President Dick Cheney, of a place that had been off the radar of most Americans for some time: Iraq. And soon we were at war with another country.

By all assessments, Iraq was a bloody and costly conflict that was poorly planned and poorly executed, not so much in the initial military campaign but in the rationale for invasion in the first place and then the management of occupation. Almost all of the press, myself included, accepted the selling of the war around "weapons of mass destruction" with far too little skepticism. The term "WMD" was a brilliant marketing campaign by the Bush administration to conflate the Armageddon scenario of a nuclear weapon (although most experts believed Iraq didn't have anywhere near the capability) with the specter of chemical weapons, which, while horrific, are much more limited in scope. This wasn't simply a vague case of "fake news." It was subtle propaganda, with just enough of an air of plausibility to lull a nation into a war of choice. And yet the press continued to use the term "WMD" up to and after the war. Meanwhile, the links of Iraq to al-Qaeda, which we now know were nonexistent, involved so much nuanced explanation of people and groups with foreign names that it was easy for the administration to sow confusion to sell its policies. And the press didn't do enough to try to explain the differences. As the military effort in Iraq became an increasingly fractious occupation, the press began to ask harder questions, despite the predictable blowback from the administration. Much of what we now know about what happened in Iraq is because of great journalism. But the policy decisions had already been made and the damage had already been done.

The war destabilized a region that was already unstable.

In the intervening years, we have seen Iran rise in power, Syria descend into a horrific civil war, and ISIS and other terrorist groups emerge. The Iraq War cost roughly forty-five hundred American lives, with thousands more severely injured, not to mention those lives lost by our allies and the large numbers of Iraqis. Estimates put the financial cost to the United States at around $2 trillion. It is a troubling lesson about the dangers of unintended consequences. And the press played a part in turning a blind eye to the government policies that were responsible for the tragedy.

In wartime, the American people tend to give an administration a lot of latitude in waging the fight, and for good reason. Wars are difficult affairs, and it is easy to be an armchair general. It is not the role of the press to suggest military strategy or to actively undercut the commander in chief. Our job is merely to ask questions, and if the answers are unsatisfactory, it is our responsibility to follow up with more questions. However, in times of strong patriotic fervor, asking a question can be spun as unpatriotic. And the Bush administration, along with its allies in the conservative press, were not hesitant to hang a "bias" sign on those who were seen as confrontational or even skeptical of the story line the administration was putting out. It wasn't overt, but there was a feeling that we shouldn't be making too many waves. Were we really going to say that the administration was playing games with reports from the intelligence community? After all, it was plausible that Saddam Hussein did have weapons of mass destruction; he had used chemical weapons in the past. Were we really going to ask too many questions about the tenuous links between Iraq and the terrorists who struck on 9/11? Wasn't Hussein a mass murderer and an avowed enemy of the United States? And when American troops are fighting in foreign fields, do you want to stand accused of not supporting them?

These are not excuses, but simply an effort to explain—however feebly—what much of the press was thinking as the Iraq War started and progressed. It must be noted that while there was wide press failure in these times, some reporters and outlets stood firm with investigative reporting that called the entire rationale for war into question. They faced tough criticism at the time, and they deserve our unmitigated appreciation.

The problems with the press leading up to and during the early years of the Iraq War were also fueled by the changing economics of the American media landscape. The business models that had sustained journalism—primarily print journalism, but also electronic media—began to crack under the stress of new technology. At the time of the Iraq War, news outlets that had already been contending with shrinking revenues, job layoffs, and general uncertainty now faced the challenges posed by the Internet. The rate at which this digital revolution has upended the model of journalism cannot be overstated. And as journalistic operations were consolidated into large corporations, reporters increasingly felt the pressure not to pursue unpopular story lines that might incur the wrath of the administration and thus harm the bottom line and shareholder value.

The technological challenges to a sustainable business model for journalism have only grown since the early years of this century. There is a lot of good, detailed scholarship on this subject, but suffice it to say that all sectors of the media have been hit hard. We have seen how online advertising has proven elusive and disappointing, and efforts such as paywalls have not proven generally effective, as consumers can readily find news online for free. Newspapers in particular have suffered. Many of the reasons that people had for maintaining their subscriptions to a paper—to check the weather and stock quotes, to get box scores and read about their favorite teams, to get a sense of the big headlines—can now all be found elsewhere, instantaneously, and also, of course, for free. Meanwhile, cash cows like classified advertisements, which used to generate billions of dollars in annual revenue for newspapers, have largely dried up thanks to sites like Craigslist. And if this environment weren't hard enough, the rise of social media as a primary news source has put further pressure on bottom lines. All these trends are important and worthy of study by those who understand the world of business far better than I do. But most important, our evolving media landscape has made it more difficult for television news networks and newspapers to have the resources to employ editors and reporters. And that has had a seismic effect on our democracy.

Simply put, we have more people talking about news and less original reporting. Whether on television or online, there is no shortage of analysis. But analysis is only as good as the information that supports it. The deep cuts to newsrooms in print and electronic media have resulted in far fewer reporters waking up each morning deciding what story they will chase. There is less investigative reporting and international coverage. At the height of CBS News, we had around twenty foreign and domestic bureaus robustly staffed. Most of those have withered or long since been shuttered. What has gotten far less attention but has perhaps been the greatest loss to our democracy is the decimation that has come to local newspapers. These were always the engines that powered much of American journalism, as great local reporting would bubble up to the national newspapers and television. Local newspapers also provided the check on local and state governments, reporting on mayors, city councils, school boards, and statehouses. This is where much of the governing of the United States takes place, but a lot of it now occurs with little or no coverage. It is as if public meetings are happening behind closed doors. And with no coverage, no one is keeping the people who work for us—on those school boards or city councils—accountable.

The promise that came with the digital age is that we would have more access to information, and that is undoubtedly true. We can read journalism from around the world, we can easily share articles with friends, and we can search for both breaking headlines and the archives of the past. But to create all this content, especially important coverage like investigative journalism, isn't free, nor is it cheap. Investigative reporters can dig for months and come up empty. Yet that is the kind of journalism that keeps our democracy honest.

I don't profess to know how to fix the business model, but I am encouraged that long-form journalism is flourishing online, from traditional outlets like the *Atlantic*, which has adapted to the digital age, to innovative, new news sites like *Vox*. And we have seen individuals with deep pockets get interested in journalism, like Amazon founder Jeff Bezos, who bought the *Washington Post*, and eBay founder Pierre Omidyar, who has given money to investigative journalism. There are many who believe that a benefactor model could be one solution, but it comes with its own vulnerabilities.

I hope we can find a sustainable means to better support online journalism, perhaps through micropayments or bundled subscriptions. And we have to connect the explosion in the consumption of news on social media to the funding of the outfits that actually do the original reporting. Anyone who cares about a free press should play a part. If you value quality journalism, support it through donations and subscriptions.

In recent years, too many of those who covered politics in Washington fell into a Beltway mindset of coziness with politicians of both parties and reporting that succumbed to false equivalence, as if every issue had two sides of equal worth. This helped pave the way for our current political situation. But I have been heartened that the press is emboldened with a newfound resilience for investigative journalism and truth-telling. There is an almost daily competition for blockbuster headlines among the *New York Times*, the *Washington Post*, and many other print and electronic outlets. This is how we have learned about cover-ups, shady dealings, bad policy, and outright lies from our elected officials. The responsible press has been hit with the ludicrous mantra of "fake news," but I believe these insults will only strengthen journalists' resolve.

Imagine where we would be today without the press working with dogged determination to hold those in power accountable. We are seeing living proof of the wisdom of our Founders, who conceived of the First Amendment as a check on tyranny—an accountability that was missing in Orwell's vision in *1984*. But while these may be heroic times for journalists, the outcome of the battle between propaganda and deception on the one hand and unbiased reporting on the other is far from clear. No one has a monopoly on the truth, but the whole premise of our democracy is that truth and justice must win out. And the role of a trained journalist is to get as close to the truth as is humanly possible. Make no mistake: We are being tested. Without a vibrant, fearless free press, our great American experiment may fail.

# COMMUNITY

★ ★ ★

# Inclusion

When I was growing up, every woman who raised me, taught me, guided me, and loved me was born into a country that did not trust her with the right to vote. African Americans were being lynched and subjected to state-sponsored segregation and disenfranchisement. Members of what we now call the LGBTQ community were nearly always referred to by the vilest of slurs, and the vast majority of them remained hidden—to society and often to themselves. People with physical challenges were pitied, but there was no systematic effort to change public buildings, transportation, sidewalks, or anything else to make the world easier for them to navigate. Jews were barred from many corridors of power. At colleges and universities, there were all sorts of restrictions on race and religion, never mind gender. Some of these were explicit and some were just understood.

America was a place where the privilege conferred on white, Protestant, straight, nondisabled men was not even questioned. This privilege remains strong today, but it now must compete with a growing chorus calling for a fairer, more inclusive nation. Legally and socially, we have made great progress, even if the summit of true equality and justice remains distant.

We often hear about how we need to be more tolerant: to make room for people, ideas, and actions with which we may not agree. This is a prerequisite for a functional democracy. But tolerance alone is not sufficient; it allows us to accept others without engaging with them, to feel smug and self-satisfied without challenging the boundaries within which too many of us live. A society worthy of our ideals would be a much more inclusive one, a more integrated one. It would be a place where we continually strive to create a better whole out of our many separate parts. This is a sentiment that itself stretches back to our founding. Our first national motto was *E pluribus unum*, "From many, one." From many states, we are one nation. And from many peoples, we should be one society. Under this framework, building tolerance is a worthy way station to a much grander destination of inclusion. This is a journey that is in our power as a nation to make. I know this to be true, because a journey from intolerance to tolerance to inclusion is one that many have made, myself included.

Back in my childhood, the idea of an African American or a woman as president was a concept so completely implausible that my peers and I never even bothered to talk about it. By the 1960s, however, the tectonic plates of American society were shifting, and I remember reporters, over adult beverages, occasionally debating whether the United States would ever have a black or female president. The consensus was a very slight maybe, some time, but none of us expected to live to see the day. It still seemed unlikely or at least in a distant future, sort of like colonizing Mars. As I look back now, it strikes me how these conversations were almost always conducted by white males only, as we made up the vast majority of the working press at the time. But in the 1960s and into the 1970s, that started to change as well. And with it, the idea of an African American or female president began to seem even more tangible. Familiarity is a necessary ingredient for acceptance.

But there was one marginalized group for whom there was almost no sense of a path to progress. If you had told us back in the 1960s and 1970s that there would be legal gay marriage in all fifty states, we would have been stunned. This was a notion that probably didn't enter even the deepest reaches of our subconscious, let alone bubble to the level of an actual concrete thought we could put into words. You couldn't ignore that there were women or African Americans in society, but you certainly could ignore the presence of gay, lesbian, bisexual, and transgender people, who most often were closeted. That such people would one day be open members of society, living with pride and having children and legal marriages? It is impossible for me to adequately convey how utterly alien those notions would have seemed.

It may be difficult for some younger readers to imagine, but for most of my life the LGBTQ community was never discussed in "polite" company. Horrible epithets for gay people were bandied about without a second thought. The very theoretical idea of someone "like that" living in your neighborhood, let alone teaching your children, was seen as a perverted threat to society. It is hard now to think back to how much this malignant ideology crossed almost all political, religious, racial, and gender boundaries. If you had asked my younger self what I thought about gay rights, I am not sure exactly what I might have said, but I am sure I would not be proud of it today. The fact that most of my peers—and even many leading progressive voices at the time—felt the same way might explain, but does not excuse, my former perspective.

In 1967, two years before the Stonewall riots in New York City would bring gay rights to national prominence, CBS News aired a documentary hosted by Mike Wallace called *The Homosexuals*. It had been years in the making and was considered one of the most controversial issues a news division could touch. The report was filled with the tropes of the times: psychiatrists claiming homosexuality was a mental condition, provocative images of hustlers, and interviews with gay Americans in anonymity, including one man with his face behind a potted plant. Wallace could state without controversy that "most Americans are repelled by the mere notion of homosexuality." He added, with a tone of journalistic certainty, "The average homosexual, if there be such, is promiscuous. He is not interested in, nor capable of, a lasting relationship like that of a heterosexual marriage. His sex life, his love life, consists of a series of chance encounters at the clubs and bars he inhabits."

I raise this not to take particular exception with Mr. Wallace. It was brave to even tackle the subject then, and the program also included sympathetic interviews with gay men talking publicly to a national audience for the first time. But the final product did not escape the deep prejudices of the times, and sadly, this ethos continued for years. When members of the gay community started getting sick with a mysterious cancer in 1981, it didn't gain much notice. At

CBS, we were one of the first news organizations to cover it, but we were still too late. At the national level, President Ronald Reagan wouldn't even utter the word "AIDS" for years. Our job as reporters, and the job of political leaders, is to confront hard truths without bias or prejudice. Unfortunately, the stigmas surrounding gay people and intravenous drug users, the two groups that initially suffered most, shaped the response from all of us.

We knew how big a story AIDS was, but there was an effort among journalists from all walks to "broaden" the reporting. When Ryan White, a young hemophiliac from Kokomo, Indiana, was diagnosed with AIDS after a blood transfusion, the disease took on a more sympathetic face for the press. It hurts my heart to write these words and think of all the thousands of gay men who suffered and died before and since. Many lived under a cloud of shame, shunned by former friends and family. In 1986, a team of reporters, including myself, did a one-hour special called *AIDS Hits Home*. It was certainly far from perfect, but it was an improvement over *The Homosexuals* from twenty years earlier. I remember interviewing a mother alongside the gay lover of her now dead son. You couldn't hear the story without being moved. But as I look back now, the subtext was that America should care more broadly about AIDS because it was no longer just a gay disease. It could infect you as well. Those were the times in which we were living, and we were not sensitive. It does bring some comfort to know that no one would cover the story in the same way today.

This societal change regarding LGBTQ rights continues to our present time. It's important to remember that as late as the Democratic primaries in the 2008 election, neither Barack Obama nor Hillary Clinton would publicly support same-sex marriage. Either they still had to "evolve" on the issue or it was considered too politically toxic. Both are now solidly pro–gay marriage, as is almost the entirety of the Democratic Party, and even many Republicans. The key, I think—and it is not a novel or original idea—is that our progress with LGBTQ rights is due to greater inclusion with the rest of society. We know that homosexuality is not limited to any race, religion, or socioeconomic class—it is part of human diversity. Once people had the courage and support to come out of the closet, families across the country, rich and poor, black and white, rural and urban, were forced to confront what had long remained hidden: sisters, brothers, sons, daughters, best friends, coworkers, even fathers and mothers, turned out to be gay, lesbian, bisexual, queer, and transgender. Now how will you respond? Will you shun them? Many did, and do, and the trails of pain, loneliness, depression, and even suicide are long and shameful. The tally of those rejected and disowned is large, and continues to grow. But thankfully many people decided to continue to love those whom they had already loved. They made room in their moral universe not only to tolerate LGBTQ people, but also to include them.

Like so many others in our country, I journeyed from ignorance to tolerance to inclusion. By the late 1990s, I had come to realize the undue challenges facing gay and lesbian people in American society, but the true burden many of them faced hadn't fully struck me. And then one day I was sitting in my office at CBS News when a longtime close colleague came in and shut the door, saying that he needed to talk to me. As soon as he sat down, he blurted out, "I'm gay." I saw in his eyes an anxiety I hadn't ever seen during our years of working together, even on the most dangerous or difficult assignments. In that moment I understood the courage it must have taken him to tell me this, and the energy he must have had to expend over the many years we had known each other to keep this central part of his life hidden.

I assured him that what he'd told me wouldn't change our relationship as coworkers and friends. As we spoke, I could see his whole demeanor shift, as if a tightly wound spring was finally allowed to relax. How can people be so blinded by prejudice as to not see the common humanity?

Thankfully, we have, as a nation and as individuals, made meaningful steps in the right directions. We must be vigilant and keep up the momentum, and there are new threats in the moment and on the horizon. Sadly, we have seen a growing movement of religious objections to same-sex marriage, with business owners denying service to gay customers. Transgender people, in particular, have not benefited from the same level of inclusion as gays and lesbians. And racial minority members of the LGBTQ community face extra levels of discrimination. But so many organizations and businesses—from the military, to government, to our major corporations—have been integrated with gays and lesbians living openly. Our society has been changed forever, and we are a stronger and more just nation because of it.

Inclusion on race has been a very different journey, and I worry that for all the progress we have made, we are stuck in the purgatory of tolerance. This may not be a comfortable thought for many who pride themselves on their progressive beliefs, but it is the truth. We have of late seen evidence of a great racial divide that remains, and in some ways even appears to be expanding, more than a half century after the major legislative victories in the civil rights movement. While tragedies like the high-profile shootings of African Americans at the hands of law enforcement get a lot of deserved attention, these are symptoms of a much deeper problem. We are still largely segregated as a society, and our political divisions increasingly fall along the lines of race. The Republican Party has become whiter and more conservative, and the Democrats have become more diverse and progressive. This shapes not only how African Americans sort politically, but increasingly Hispanics and Asians too. Yes, we saw a historic moment in the 2008 election with our first African American president, but how distant all the talk of a "post-racial America" seems today. The election of President Barack Obama was a mark of progress, but the racist and demeaning comments from some of his critics (like the lies about his birth certificate) during his presidency highlighted the intransigent lines of division that remain within our society. This environment has only intensified since President Obama left office, as a political climate of greater polarization now emanates from the highest levels of government. The long shadow of slavery, segregation, and racism still looms over this nation.

Several years ago I worked on a documentary on the public school system of Detroit. The city has become a potent symbol of so many of the challenges that face this country, race being first and foremost. But for the children growing up in the poverty and hopelessness of much of Detroit today, symbolism doesn't matter. This is their one and only chance at a life, and the historical, political, sociological, psychological, legal, and other headwinds they face seem disproportionate and cruel. The documentary found a broken city of families struggling against the odds of deserted neighborhoods, inadequate public transportation, and low-paying jobs. Meanwhile the school system has been plagued by corruption and mismanagement.

Amid all this, one truth cannot be ignored: The Detroit public schools are almost entirely African American, and the schools in the surrounding suburbs are overwhelmingly white. This is not an accident. In 1974, the Supreme Court heard a case that centered on Detroit's schools, both in the city and in the surrounding communities. In *Milliken v. Bradley*, the court ruled in a 5–4 decision that a metropolis could in essence be segregated along district lines, just not within those districts. In other words, it was okay if there were real racial divisions, lines of exclusion, between suburbs and cities. And that is the system we largely have today. When you hear the term "inner-city schools," close your eyes and picture the student body. Now picture a suburban school. I am pretty sure that race was part of your mental image. This is not a mirage. Recent governmental and academic studies have shown increased de facto school segregation in the last few decades. In a blistering dissent to the *Milliken* decision, the first African American justice on the Supreme Court, Thurgood Marshall, predicted our current reality: "School district lines, however innocently drawn, will surely be perceived as fences to separate the races." We have become a less inclusive nation as a result.

In our reporting for the documentary, I interviewed a remarkable young woman named Deanna Williams, who was a high school student at the time. In the emotional apex of our conversation, with tears streaming down her face, she explained the very human cost of this segregation. When she watched TV news about suburban schools, she saw resources aplenty. But in Detroit, they had very little. "It's frustrating to know that I could be learning all of these things and I could be doing all of these things, and I can't," Deanna told me. "And people think . . . that the children in the Detroit Public Schools are stupid and brutish because of what they see on television. And it's not true. We want to learn. We want to be able to do what the other children are doing. We want to have the same opportunities. But they keep taking them away from us. They keep—it's like they're keeping us down! . . . And every day I want to know why. Why is this happening?"

We titled the film *A National Disgrace*, not only because of the deep dysfunction of the Detroit schools, but because we as a nation allowed this to happen. And studies have shown that some of the most segregated school districts are in the most liberal cities—like New York and San Francisco. What lessons are we teaching our children? We may support social programs that we think help those who are disadvantaged or who have faced discrimination, but if we do not fully engage in a spirit of inclusion on a personal level, we are failing. We live largely separated from one another, and most people seem to be okay with that. It is not good enough to vote for politicians who will do the right thing on racial issues, or even to give money to worthy causes. If we are not actively trying to tear down the "fences to separate the races," as Justice Marshall described it, then we are all part of the problem.

Building a more inclusive nation for women presents a unique set of hurdles (keeping in mind that LGBTQ women and women from racial minorities face multiple forms of discrimination). We have made great strides. But I worry deeply that the biases against women have proven difficult to identify and correct within individuals. And this condition doesn't apply only to men; I have known many women who have great talent and intelligence but who diminish themselves in accordance with the expectations of society at large.

The struggles women face in achieving equality remain both legal and cultural. In 2007, my reporting team and I investigated a story of female and minority custodians in the New York City public schools who claimed they had faced discrimination in the early 1990s. Of the nearly 900 custodians, 92 percent were white, and only 12 individuals were women. The Civil Rights Division of the Department of Justice brought suit in 1996. But when New York City agreed to a settlement, a group of white male custodians sued, claiming reverse discrimination. The American Civil Liberties Union became involved to look out for the rights of the female and minority custodians, but a final resolution wasn't reached until 2014, when a federal judge gave final approval to another settlement that seemed to address the concerns of all the parties. This story is a reminder that often the plights of women and minorities are linked, and that justice is often delayed if not denied.

The division of the ACLU that had taken up the custodians' case was the Women's Rights Project, which was co-founded by Ruth Bader Ginsburg in the early '70s. Ginsburg directed the unit until she joined the federal bench in 1980, and during her time at the ACLU, in a series of landmark cases before the Supreme Court, she ushered in a new era of law for gender discrimination. It was something she had experienced firsthand: As one of only a handful of female law students at Harvard, she was denied a clerkship to the Supreme Court because of her gender, and after graduating tied for first in her class from Columbia Law School, she was not offered a single job by a law firm. Inspired by the civil rights movement, Ginsburg decided to join the ACLU and use the legal system to tackle the injustices facing women in American society. "Our strategy was the soul of simplicity," Ginsburg has said. "It was to go after the stereotypes that were written into law."

When Ginsburg was nominated to the Supreme Court in 1993, 106 justices had preceded her, and only one, the trailblazer Sandra Day O'Connor, had been a woman. I met Justice Ginsburg recently in her chambers, and to be in her presence is to feel that she is a quintessential Supreme Court justice. She is thoughtful, wise, and clearly blessed with a brilliant mind that has been honed and shaped through years of scholarship. It is hard to remember that because of her gender, for most of American history almost no one would have thought of her as even a small-town lawyer, let alone a Supreme Court justice.

There is no doubt that having women on the bench has had a profound effect. In 2009, the court heard a case involving the strip search of a thirteen-year-old girl. At the time, Ginsburg was the only woman on the court, and during the oral arguments of the case, many of the justices expressed skepticism as to whether the girl's rights had been violated. "They have never been a thirteen-year-old girl,"

Justice Ginsburg explained to *USA Today*. "It's a very sensitive age for a girl. I didn't think that my colleagues, some of them, quite understood." It is believed that Justice Ginsburg set out to make sure her colleagues understood. In a result that surprised many court watchers, the justices ruled 8–1 in favor of the girl. This is the power of inclusion.

The more we are around people with a variety of life experiences, the more we can understand and value the needs and worth of our fellow citizens. But our own life experiences can also shape our views. In 2003, the conservative chief justice William Rehnquist issued a ruling upholding the Family and Medical Leave Act for state employers, a decision Justice Ginsburg called "such a delightful surprise" in an interview with the *New York Times*. Chief Justice Rehnquist had shown skepticism of such issues in the past, but Justice Ginsburg attributed his change of heart to the facts of his own life. "When his daughter Janet was divorced, I think the chief felt some kind of responsibility to be kind of a father figure to those girls [his grandchildren]. So he became more sensitive to things that he might not have noticed."

In many ways, we have made important legal progress when it comes to women. As the proud father of a daughter who came of age in the wake of a growing feminist movement, I saw how she benefited, as did many students and athletes, from the famous Title IX of the Education Amendments Act of 1972. That act stated: "No person in the United States shall, on the basis of sex, be excluded from participation in, be denied the benefits of, or be subjected to discrimination under any education program or activity receiving Federal financial assistance." But it's one thing to have greater equality of opportunity under the law (itself an elusive goal), and another to see it happen in practice. How do we modify a work environment to better acknowledge the biological realities of pregnancy, childbirth, and the need for day care? How do we counteract the shaming of women according to how they look or act when we see case after case of a reinforced gender hierarchy in our media, on Wall Street and Main Street, in Silicon Valley, and from some of our highest elected officials? How do we ward off the subtle undertow of the prevalent belief that women are not good in science and math, which can lead to what social scientists call the "stereotype threat"? These are not easy questions, and they defy easy solutions. But as society has gotten more inclusive, we can no longer ignore them. And that, in itself, is a form of progress.

When I was young, we heard often of how the United States was a great melting pot. It is a fine metaphor as far as it goes. But inclusion, not assimilation, should be the key concept in seeking, ever seeking, a more perfect national union. Our own history has shown that we are stronger as a mosaic than a melting pot. Our nation is bound together more by ideals than by blood or land, and inclusion is in our cultural DNA. We should feel proud that we are not all the same, and that we can share our differences under the common umbrella of humanity. To do so, we must confront the voices of intolerance and come to terms with our own complicity in condoning the divisions in our society. We have seen that progress is possible, within ourselves and the nation at large. But it requires perseverance, hard work, and a commitment to respect the dignity of all who call America home.

# Empathy

I am not sure if the word "empathy" was in either of my parents' vocabularies. It wasn't the kind of word one heard growing up in my neighborhood in Houston. But my parents taught me about the importance of empathy through their words and deeds. And they made it clear that it was part of the glue that held together our family, our neighborhood, our community, and the United States itself.

My earliest memories are of times of despair and the Great Depression. Our family home was on Prince Street, on the extreme outer edge of what was the Houston of the 1930s. It was more of a big town back then, not yet really a city. We lived in the Heights neighborhood, which today is hip and gentrified, but back then our street was just a lightly

graveled road. It was considered a rough, tough neighborhood, and there was only one street—a dirt street—between
our house and the open country. Across that road was a
large field, a creek, and, beyond that, a densely wooded pine
forest. I thought of it as the Great American Frontier, and
the truth was, in those days before interstate highways, you
might have been able to find a path to walk from the end
of my block to the Canadian border without seeing many,
if any, other travelers.

Our house was nothing to brag about, but at least it had
four sturdy walls, with two bedrooms, a small living room,
a small kitchen, and one bath. My brother and I shared a
bed, and my sister slept in the same room until she got a
little older, when my father and uncle added a small room
to the house. Across our street was a poor frame house in a
state of semicollapse. A half block down lived a family who
didn't even have a house, just a corrugated tin roof held up
by four posts in the corners and one in the middle. Their
floor was dirt.

Nobody in either of these families had a job. That was
not unusual in our neighborhood during the Depression.
And the families that were lucky enough to have work usually had only meager part-time jobs. A full-time job like
the one my father had working the oil fields was rare and
considered a blessing, no matter the pay, the hours, or the

amount of backbreaking labor it entailed. This was what the United States of America was like not that long ago: a country where families struggled to live on dirt streets, with dirt floors and little or no income to pay the grocery or medical bills. None of this was considered particularly unusual at the time. It was just the way things were.

The father of the family in the dilapidated house had lost a leg. Exactly how he'd lost it was unclear, but the prevailing belief was that it had happened after a misjudged leap from a boxcar. Riding the rails was not uncommon then as a means to get to your destination, but it was uncommonly dangerous. His condition brought a crushing change to his fortune and that of his family. Before the accident, the father had been a day laborer for hire, a man with a shovel who could dig you a ditch. But there wasn't much demand for a one-legged ditchdigger. He had likely not gotten good medical attention after the accident, and I remember him clearly as a frail man with a bad cough. He, his wife, and their four or five children had no money. Zero. They eventually applied for some form of relief, but it came only sporadically.

The family under the tin roof had a passel of kids as well, maybe as many as six. I remember thinking how elderly the father was, although he was probably much younger than he looked. A hard life will do that to a person. For some reason this other family, despite their abject poverty, didn't seem to qualify for the government's new "relief" program (otherwise known as "the dole"). Perhaps they didn't know how to fill out the paperwork. Public support was far less systematic than it is today. Around the neighborhood, this family had a reputation for often being in prayer, and as a boy I wondered how God could be so seemingly blind to such suffering.

The neighborhood tried as best it could to help these families stay alive. If we had leftovers after supper, we would walk them across the street. One of my earliest impressions was taking that short journey with my father. You might think that these families were humiliated by the offerings, but there is no dignity in being hungry. And there was no judgment or disdain on the part of those offering assistance. No one wondered why those neighbors weren't working, and no one passed moral judgments on their inability to fend for themselves. We understood that, in life, some are dealt aces, some tens, and some deuces.

Food wasn't the only assistance we provided. One morning I watched my uncle John dig a ditch from our house across the gravel road to the ramshackle house. The family had been unable to pay their water bills, and my uncle was good with pipes. So he connected the two houses, and we shared our water with them. These acts of kindness were also not unusual among neighbors. Necessity was a great motivator for innovation and empathy.

On Christmas Eve, my father and uncle pooled their money, meager though it was, and bought toys for the families living in the dilapidated house and under the tin roof. I remember a rag doll, a small wooden train, and for some reason a tambourine—why these details are so vivid I couldn't say. We waited until after the children had gone to bed to give the gifts quietly to the parents, so that when those children woke up the next morning they would not think Santa had forsaken them. That was the hope, anyway.

What sticks with me more than even that act of kindness was how my mother talked to me about it. I was an inquisitive child (perhaps not surprising considering my later path in life), and I was always asking questions. So I asked my mother why we gave those families gifts at Christmas when we ourselves didn't have much. I remember then answering for myself: "It was because we felt sorry for them, right?"

"We do not feel sorry for them," my mother said sternly. "We understand how they feel." It was a lesson that is so seared in my mind, I can see her face and I can hear her tone of voice as if it were yesterday.

What my family did was not heroic. I like to think of it more as neighborly. And it was in line with a national ethos in those dark days, repeated countless times in countless communities across the country. We understood that those who were suffering weren't lazy or lacking the desire to do better. Fate had the potential to slap any of us. In another family in our neighborhood, the father had a part-time job as a watchman. One morning a neighbor noticed that he had come home from work early, and then she saw his wife crying. When she went over to find out what had happened, she learned the man had lost his job. The news spread from neighbor to neighbor like an unwired telegraph. By the time my father came home from work, people were gathering to grieve with the unlucky family. Their house had the feeling of one mourning the death of a loved one. Everybody knew that a lost job was not likely to be replaced.

There is one other story that for me is perhaps the most resonant. It is of a boy, a few years older than I, who lived near us and had a gifted artistic sensibility. He was the kind of kid who could draw almost anything. I remember, with wonder, how he could build model airplanes out of balsa wood with perfect symmetry and not a wrinkle in the paper skins that covered them. In different circumstances, he might have grown up to show his work in galleries. He had also been a strong student and a wonderful athlete, winning all the footraces in the neighborhood and dominating sandlot football. His love for the Glenn Miller Orchestra irked some of his neighbors, who complained about how many times he played the three records he owned. But his family was in dire economic straits, so he quit school at fifteen to start looking for a job to support them.

He never found much work other than a few projects helping out a bricklayer. What he did start to find was trouble. He began smoking and running with the wrong crowd. He started hanging out on the street corners, often late into the night. Before long, he became ill with what I believe was some respiratory ailment and went into the hospital. When I visited him, I saw the shell of a young man, in many ways still a boy. I had looked up to him as one blessed with talent and grace, and here he was, completely defeated by a life that had once held such promise. Shortly thereafter he died. I attributed it to a broken heart and I imagine him taking his final breaths with flashes of what could have been, what might have been.

It is perhaps not surprising that Nazi Germany and Imperial Japan looked at a nation so traumatized and felt they could defeat us. Of course, history turned out differently. The same generation that had been driven to such depths in the 1930s rose up to push back the forces of totalitarianism in a two-ocean global war in the 1940s. Perhaps those authoritarians, who felt no empathy for their own people or those they conquered, underestimated the strength of our empathy. Empathy builds community. Communities strengthen a country and its resolve and will to fight back. We were never as unified in national purpose as we were in those days. What had weakened us had also made us stronger.

I remember a major push to organize for civil defense, as there was great fear of a German or Japanese invasion. Almost everyone, truly everyone, regardless of age, race, or economic status, rushed to come together and help as soon as word came out. Our neighborhood wasn't known for organization, but this need galvanized even those you would have never expected to volunteer. We practiced blackouts, and people were deputized as air raid wardens. It might seem a little silly now, but we all took this very seriously. It must be noted, of course, that we were still a segregated nation. But the war effort, including the service of African American soldiers, helped change the country in that regard as well. In 1948, President Harry Truman would desegregate the armed forces, six years before *Brown v. Board of Education* ended segregation in our public schools.

Indeed, this sweep of empathy continued after the war. One of the best foreign policy efforts in American history was to help rebuild Europe and Japan. Our enemies became our friends through an acknowledgment of the common bonds of humanity. The postwar world order was built on that foundation. And when the GIs returned home, we treated them empathetically as well. The Servicemen's

Readjustment Act of 1944, more commonly known as the GI Bill, was one of the greatest pieces of social legislation in our nation's history. Among other benefits, the GI Bill ensured that servicemen's tuitions to college or technical school were fully paid. Empathy makes for wise foreign and domestic policy.

When I consider the forces that have led to our greatest moments of progress, I do not think it is a surprise that a great spasm of empathetic legislation came in the midst of the Great Depression. The beginning of Social Security is the most notable example, but there were a host of other programs that aimed to bring relief and the dignity of work to a populace in desperate need. Many of these endeavors fell under the so-called alphabet agencies, federal programs created by President Franklin Roosevelt to combat the Great Depression. One of the most consequential was the WPA (Works Progress Administration), which at its height employed millions of people on public works projects across the country. But there were also programs like the TVA (Tennessee Valley Authority), which brought electrification and other services to a particularly hard-hit area of the country; the SEC (Securities and Exchange Commission), which regulated the stock market and other financial exchanges; and the FLSA (Fair Labor Standards Act), which established the minimum wage, overtime pay, and child labor rules. The last three of these programs remain an example of the enduring legacy of that time. This effort was widely popular and seen as the worthy and necessary actions of a government in touch with the needs of the people it served.

The second wave of such legislation came in the 1960s, and I don't think it is coincidental that this happened as the children of the Great Depression and World War II grew into adulthood. Efforts to improve racial justice, labor rights, antipoverty programs, education, medical care, and many other needs began under President John F. Kennedy's "New Frontier" and peaked with President Lyndon Johnson's "Great Society." The scope of the legislation from this time is still staggering: the Civil Rights Act, the Voting Rights Act, Medicare, Medicaid, among others. Note that most of these laws were passed with considerable—sometimes overwhelming—bipartisan support. My generation came of age in a period marked by firsthand knowledge of what it was like to be faced with economic despair and a brutal war. We knew of no other world than one of hardship, and so we did not realize growing up how dire and anomalous the situation was. I cannot imagine there was a more conducive environment in which to learn the lessons of empathy.

Today these kinds of empathetic programs are associated with big government bureaucracies. There are legitimate questions about the manner in which they operate, and they could probably be improved. It is undeniable that they still do good work in bringing more fairness and justice to our democracy, but the spirit of empathy with which they were created has been lost. Empathy is a deeply personal emotion. It is about the feeling one has for one's fellow human beings. Transferring responsibilities to government is often necessary, but it creates a distance between us and those who need help. And if this impulse of forgoing our individual responsibilities is left unchecked, it absolves us from our own responsibility as citizens to form a more empathetic union with others.

I worry that our nation today suffers from a deficit of empathy, and this is especially true of many in positions of national leadership. It is a phenomenon that is born from, and that exacerbates, the broader divisions tearing at our republic. We see a rising tribalism along cultural, ethnic, economic class, and geographic lines. And the responsibility for these divisions should fall more squarely on the shoulders of the powerful, those who need to be empathetic, than on those who need our empathy. When we live in a self-selected bubble of friends, neighbors, and colleagues, it is too easy to forget how important it is to try to walk in the shoes of others. Technology and social media can be tools for connecting us, but I fear these advancements are in many ways deepening and hardening the divisions between us.

Very few families escaped the wounds of the Great Depression and World War II. In the intervening decades, however, the wealthy and the powerful largely have been protected from economic, social, and military upheavals by a shield of immunity. A commonality of understanding has been lost. Where once the American experience was one of a spectrum from the rich to the poor, now we live in pockets that insulate us from others. We have more in the ranks of the extremely wealthy, many fewer in the middle economic class, and a larger pool falling further and further behind. So we grow more isolated and less empathetic. The threads stitching our union together begin to fray. We see others, but we cannot imagine what their lives are actually like. We don't even think we should have to bother.

Empathy is not only a personal feeling; it can be a potent force for political and social change. And thus the suppression or denial of empathy is a deliberate part of a cynical political calculus. Dividing people and stoking animosity can pave a path to power (and in many recent elections, it has). This has been well known since the time of the ancients. But these divisions inevitably come at the expense of the long-term health and welfare of the nation as a whole. We have seen many examples from our history where the economic and social needs of one group have been pitted against another's—on immigration, labor rights, environmental protections, racial justice, and so many more. Such clashes usually do not end very well. In contrast, there have been moments where we reached out to one another as a nation, channeling what unites us rather than what separates us. It might be hard to imagine today, but there were times when the common purpose of the United States seemed to rise above pettiness and narrow self-interest.

One often finds the greatest lack of empathy in those who were born lucky. They tend to misidentify that luck as the superiority of their character. There are some notable exceptions: The incredibly successful investor Warren Buffett once speculated to a group of students about what would happen if, before birth, a genie gave us the opportunity to choose the political, economic, and social system into which we would be born. "What's the catch?" he said. "One catch—just before you emerge [from the womb] you have to go through a huge bucket with seven billion slips, one for each human. Dip your hand in and that is what you get—you could be born intelligent or not intelligent, born healthy or disabled, born black or white, born in the U.S. or in Bangladesh, etc. You have no idea which slip you will get. Not knowing which slip you are going to get, how would you design the world?"

It is a wonderful thought experiment that lays out a provocative case for empathy. Buffett calls his construct "the ovarian lottery." Now, take a moment to imagine the most sanctimonious of our current national voices. Imagine those who lecture most loudly about morality and personal responsibility from the perch of privilege. Imagine those who blame the victims of discrimination and poverty. How would these men and women fare in such a lottery as Buffett outlines? What would their message be if they themselves had been born under far different circumstances? These people are in dire need of humility, a humility bathed in the refreshing waters of empathy. We can all afford to drink more from that spring as well.

# Immigration

No one can deny that the United States is now, and has always been, a nation of immigrants, even if the issue of immigration has become one of the most contentious and divisive of our current age. And yet, improbable as it may sound, I don't remember hearing the word "immigrant" until I was in early adulthood. It was likely because of a quirk in history and geography. For one, my childhood during the Great Depression and World War II marked one of the lowest ebbs of foreign arrivals to our shores in our nation's history. And also the Texas of my youth seemed to me at the time so overwhelmingly white and Protestant that it was hard to imagine any other type of America.

Of course it wasn't really white. Houston also contained

a significant population of African Americans, but they lived separate, segregated lives, and very little attention was paid in my school or upbringing to the means by which their ancestors had arrived in the Americas. There were also many Mexicans in Houston, but we never really considered them immigrants so much as the cultural backdrop of Texas. The southern border of the United States was not far away, and nobody paid it much heed at the time. We all knew that it could be easily crossed from both sides for purposes of work and pleasure. I remember Mexican children, the sons and daughters of migrant farmworkers, starting each fall at my elementary school. By the time we got to Thanksgiving, the harvest and livestock roundups were complete, and all of those schoolmates would be gone.

There were undoubtedly small immigrant communities in Houston—Irish and Italian populations, Catholics and Jews—but none of these groups made a sizable impression on my young consciousness.

But later, when I was wooing my wife, Jean, I traveled out to meet her family in the deep hinterland of Texas. This was about as far as one could get from people's perceptions of immigrant America—the Lower East Side of New York City, the ethnic neighborhoods of the midwestern cities, the Chinatowns of the West. Hers was a place of open vistas, where the scrub oaks far outnumbered the human inhabitants. But Jean was a descendant of a hardy immigrant stock that still harbored a strong sense of their transatlantic journey, one made many decades earlier.

Jean came from a people known as the Wends, a Lutheran minority of Slavic ancestry who had been living in Germany and had faced cultural and religious persecution. In the days of the Texas Republic, before it joined the United States (1836–1845), the government in Austin commissioned agents in Europe to encourage immigrants to populate their young nation. One thing Texas had in abundance was land, and its government was promising large tracts to immigrants who would settle on the frontier (I imagine they made little mention of the existing Native American population). The story goes that this appeal made a big impression on a congregation of Wends, and a few families made the arduous journey to the U.S. They sent back glowing reports of vast horizons, of both geography and opportunity. This was enough for the entire congregation to make the dangerous passage across the great Atlantic in the mid-nineteenth century. Many died of disease en route, but the ones who survived landed in Galveston and spread inland. Many set up communities in towns so small they consisted of just a few families. Jean's hometown of Winchester had a population that could be counted in the few dozens.

As I got to know Jean's family, I began to revel in the

great immigrant currents that had shaped the United States more broadly. I saw how this was a continent that beckoned to the poor and persecuted from around the globe with offers of freedom and seemingly boundless space. For much of the relatively short history of the United States, most of the world still lived under the remnants of feudal systems. The United States offered a destiny of one's own making.

From Jean's relatives, I learned that moving here did not require erasing a pride in one's ancestry. While the Wends had embraced their American identity, they still felt strongly affiliated with the cultural taproots of the old country. It struck me at times that their journey to America seemed to have happened in the recent past, even though not one of Jean's living family members had known a home other than the challenging Texas prairie. And I saw how thoroughly these families embraced their American identity—they were patriots, just like the people with whom I had grown up. But they also understood that they were from another continent. This is one of the greatest lessons of our nation's improbable makeup: A united citizenry can be quilted together from so many different cultural fabrics. I was already in my twenties, but I was realizing I had a lot to learn about a country I loved deeply.

We all have come here from somewhere else, and the vast majority of us are only a few generations removed from another land. Whether that is one generation or ten, it seems rather sanctimonious to claim that there is much of a difference. Not many of us can trace our arrival back a few hundred years, let alone millennia. But even the ancestors of the Native Americans are believed to have come across a land bridge from Asia—a reminder that we are a species of migrations, and always have been. Of course, not all migrations have been voluntary; many are here because their ancestors were ripped from their homelands in Africa and carried across the ocean in bondage.

Too many times the term "American" has been used as a weapon against new immigrants, especially those who look, speak, or pray differently. And yet one of the noblest ideals of our country is that anybody from anywhere can be an American. This has been, and continues to be, an eternal battle between our demons and angels for the soul of the United States. And it was present at the baptism of a nation that proclaimed "all men are created equal" but defined many men as three-fifths of a whole, never mind women of all races.

The debate over immigration takes many forms, and some of them are worth considering. We are a land of opportunity and prosperity, and it would be wonderful if we had the ability to welcome everyone seeking a better life to our shores. We cannot, so we will always have to make hard choices. There are also many hard questions. How do we handle undocumented immigrants, not only the ones who have crossed our southern border, but also those who have overstayed visas? How do we continue to welcome skilled workers who can benefit our economy without taking jobs away from American citizens capable of doing the work but who might demand a higher wage? How do we contend with the fact that many undocumented workers do difficult and dangerous jobs, in agriculture, construction, and service, that most Americans do not seem to want to do themselves? How do we balance empathy for refugees seeking asylum with security concerns? Immigration will always be a complicated and perplexing issue, especially if we remain a country that is perceived as a promised land. That is the spirit that drew most of our ancestors, and hopefully we will remain such a nation.

As we all know, however, the immigration debate isn't only about policy and economics; it is also about culture, race, and religion. We are at a particularly ugly juncture in this regard, but we have been here before. In the early days of the republic, the country needed settlers, so nearly anyone could immigrate. Then, as the United States started to grow and be seen as a land of opportunity, a big wave of immigration began in the decades before the Civil War. Most were from Northern and Central Europe, and many were

Catholics—particularly from Germany and Ireland. This sparked a fierce backlash and the rise of the American Party, nicknamed the Know-Nothing Party. Its ranks were driven largely by anti-immigrant and anti-Catholic sentiments. The ugly echoes of their intolerance can be heard today, and it is ironic that some who question the "Americanness" of more recent arrivals are themselves descendants of those who were labeled "un-American" in the nineteenth century.

In the mid-1800s, the United States also saw an influx of immigrants from China, drawn by the rush for gold in California and the need for labor and entrepreneurial energy that accompanied the miners. Even though Chinese laborers undertook the dangerous work of the western half of the transcontinental railroad, discrimination against them was intense. In 1882, Congress passed the Chinese Exclusion Act, which barred Chinese laborers from entering the United States. Japanese immigration expanded to fill labor demand no longer being provided by Chinese immigrants, and it grew rapidly after the turn of the century up and down the Pacific coast. But a so-called gentleman's agreement between the U.S. and Japanese governments soon limited formal immigration from that country as well.

At the same time, new waves of immigrants were hitting the eastern shores from Southern and Eastern Europe, including millions of Catholics and Jews. This shift in the makeup of the United States citizenry sparked an effort to make America look more like it once did. Congress passed sharp quotas on immigration in the 1920s, favoring people from Northern Europe, which set the stage for one of the most shameful chapters in our history. As refugees started to pour out of Europe to escape fascism, the United States tightened its borders and even turned some ships away, sending men, women, and children back to their deaths.

This xenophobia at the time of World War II also affected how Americans viewed their fellow citizens. The internment of over a hundred thousand Japanese Americans came from misplaced fears that they might sabotage the war effort. Fear has often been a powerful motivator for exclusion and persecution. German Americans were ostracized—and some even detained—during the First World War (much less so during World War II). These days, Muslims find themselves particularly under attack, not only by discriminatory new government immigration policies but also in schools, public spaces, and other avenues of daily life where their fellow citizens often make negative assumptions about their religion and reasons for being here. Never mind that immigrants are rarely responsible for violent acts. Seldom do they attempt to undermine the values of our country.

Instead, we have seen time and again that immigrants and their children are eager to serve their new nation, and often at great sacrifice. While Japanese Americans were being interned during World War II, an infantry regiment was formed of Japanese American soldiers—mostly the sons of immigrants from Hawaii. Because of the sheer numbers of Japanese Americans living in Hawaii, it was unfeasible to send most of them to internment camps (demonstrating the capriciousness of the policy). Thousands of young Japanese American men enlisted in what became known as the 442nd Regimental Combat Team. The 442nd saw fierce fighting in Europe and is, by some estimations, the most decorated group of soldiers in American history. As a Texan, I was keenly aware of their service when, in October 1944, they rescued the so-called Lost Battalion (a unit of the Texas National Guard), which had been surrounded by the Nazi army in the Vosges Mountains of France. After a hellacious winter battle, 211 of the 275 men in the Lost Battalion walked out alive, while the 442nd suffered 800 dead and wounded in the fight.

In recent years, when I reported from distant and dangerous military outposts in Iraq and Afghanistan, I saw a great diversity of surnames stitched into uniforms—and the pride of service in diverse faces. It was renewed proof that we are a nation of immigrants who believe in service. I have had a similar experience reading the names etched into marble in Arlington National Cemetery. Patriotism and sacrifice know no ethnicity, race, or religion. And it has always been thus. Whether it's the more than 40 percent of the Union soldiers in the Civil War who were born overseas or had a parent who was an immigrant, or the late Humayun Khan, a U.S. Army captain who died in a suicide attack in Iraq and then became a potent symbol in our current political debate, there should be no question about whether our newest Americans are willing to sacrifice for their adopted country.

When I moved to New York in 1962, most of the immigration was still European. Certain nationalities coalesced around certain trades, and I found that the soundmen's union was almost exclusively Eastern European (they would often merge German and English, saying "*mit*out sound" instead of "without sound"). The cameramen seemed to be mostly Irish, and there were all sorts of other accents I had never heard before. Around the CBS newsroom, at drinks after work, and out on assignment, much of our banter was hardly politically correct, and there was a lot of ethnic stereotyping in our jokes. But I remember being struck by how collegial it all felt. In the news business, like the army, you can't get much done if you don't work together.

This was also the first time I really got to know Jewish Americans, starting when Bernie Birnbaum took me under his wing. He was different from me in every way imaginable—

native New Yorker, the son of Russian immigrants, Fulbright Scholar. We instantly became dear friends. Bernie was a fast talker, and I remember struggling to keep up with his flow of words, and his accent. I had never even heard of kosher food, so Bernie took me to the famed Carnegie Deli, where he explained the concept in the midst of a sea of tables filled with other fast talkers. Bernie had nothing for clothes and his socks would sometimes be mismatched. In my naïveté, I remember thinking this was what all Jewish people were like. Ernie Leiser, who had hired me after seeing my coverage of Hurricane Carla for the CBS affiliate in Houston, was everything Bernie was not: well tailored, calm, and soft-spoken. I had no idea that he was also Jewish until Bernie told me. I was learning that real people didn't fall neatly into stereotypes, a lesson that many need to revisit these days.

The immigrant spirit that coursed through the hallways of CBS News was seen as one of our core strengths. Blair Clark, the vice president of CBS News, was about as traditional American stock as you could get, Harvard-educated from a prominent white Protestant family. But he was a true progressive and would later become editor of the *Nation* magazine. With a nod to the dapper CBS News correspondents of the day, Clark advised me to "dress British and think Yiddish" if I wanted to be successful. A comment like this might seem offensive or anachronistic in today's world, but I certainly don't think that was his intention and it was not how I took it.

What we didn't know at the time was that a sea change was coming that would transform the United States forever. On October 3, 1965, President Lyndon Johnson traveled to Liberty Island in the harbor of New York and signed a sweeping change to America's immigration laws. At the feet of the monumental statue that had welcomed so many of the huddled masses to our shores, Johnson undid a system that had been in place since the anti-immigrant backlash of the 1920s.

The new law eliminated immigration quotas based on race, ethnicity, and nation of origin. Instead, it set up different preferential criteria, such as having a relative who was a U.S. citizen or legal resident and working in a profession with specialized skills. Johnson framed the bill in rousing language: "[The old system] violated the basic principle of American democracy—the principle that values and rewards each man on the basis of his merit as a man. . . . Our beautiful America was built by a nation of strangers. From a hundred different places or more they have poured forth into an empty land, joining and blending in one mighty and irresistible tide."

For all the soaring rhetoric, there was a feeling at the time that this 1965 law would not change America too drastically. (Johnson himself said it was "not a revolutionary bill.") The preference for immigrants with family members already living in the United States was seen by many as a way to ensure that a predominantly white country stay that way. In reality it has had the opposite effect, as individuals from Asia, Africa, the Caribbean, South America, and many other far-flung locations have immigrated to the United States, and their extended families have followed. The resulting change in American demographics has been revolutionary. According to the Pew Research Center, in 1965, 84 percent of Americans were non-Hispanic white. By 2015, that number had dropped to 62 percent. And they estimate that "by 2055, the U.S. will not have a single racial or ethnic majority." That is a staggering shift. Think about the paintings of our Founding Fathers, the presidential portraits, the old black-and-white newsreels and photographs of Americans at work and play. The faces in all of those are predominantly white. That America is fading, and we will become more diverse in the future.

Over the course of our nation's history, waves of immigration have time and again expanded the definition of what it means to be an American. And each time, eras of permissive immigration were bracketed by eras of deep restrictions. Those who wished to bar the Eastern and Southern Europeans, the Chinese, the Japanese, the Mexicans, the Catholics, the Jews, and now the Muslims and so many others have all used some version of the same argument: America will no longer be America.

They have always been wrong. We have attracted some of the best scientists and inventors and entrepreneurs and artists and athletes and every other category you can think of because we are a place where people of all kinds can be Americans.

But we cannot deny that change can create feelings of anxiety and unease among those who see America, as they know it, slipping away. We should not succumb to bigotry, but we should also have empathy for those who are worried about their future. There are legitimate concerns, but if politicians of all persuasions tried to speak to audiences beyond their own voting base and argued that we must root for prosperity among all Americans, I suspect much of this anxiety could be diminished. That can't happen easily or quickly. It will require time and tolerance. It is one of our most difficult challenges of the twenty-first century.

We have been able to reach consensus on immigration, even relatively recently. In 1986 President Ronald Reagan oversaw the passage of a bill that allowed millions of people living in this country without documentation to come out of the shadows. Two years earlier, President Reagan had said, in a presidential debate against Walter Mondale, "I believe in the idea of amnesty for those who have put down roots and who have lived here even though sometime back they may have entered illegally." Imagine: The patron saint of the modern conservative movement made the case for a concept that today would have him pilloried by the right-wing press and those cynical politicians who have learned to exploit division for their own electoral success. But with the right leadership, I believe we could find similar compromise today.

I remember a moment late in the 2008 presidential campaign when Barack Obama returned to his birth state of Hawaii for a vacation. Some pundits criticized this decision for the optics, arguing that our fiftieth state might strike some voters as exotic and foreign. At the same time, there was also a candidate on the ballot from the forty-ninth state, Alaska governor Sarah Palin. The glaciers and tundra of the Last Frontier are just as exotic as the beaches and palm trees of Hawaii, but I don't remember hearing that Alaska was somehow bad for campaign optics. What I think was at issue wasn't geography but race. Hawaii is the most diverse state in the Union, the result of waves of Asian immigration. By contrast, Alaska is predominantly white, save for a considerable population of Native Americans.

These states are two of the most marvelous and welcoming in our nation. Their natural wonders are matched only by the friendliness of their inhabitants, and I have enjoyed my time in both immensely. But when you look at the demographic trends of the United States, Alaska is more a throwback to the past, and Hawaii a glimpse of the future. We are destined to look and live more like Hawaii, a multiethnic society where racial lines are blurred through intermarriage, and cultural heritages combine into a new America. Even my hometown of Houston is now one of the most ethnically diverse cities in the country.

Today we see an eagerness among some of our elected officials—buoyed by passionate segments of the voting public—to erect new barriers to immigration. But these efforts will not stop the demographic momentum already underway in the United States. If anything, I believe that demonizing the most recent arrivals to our shores will only, over time, galvanize the political will of the majority of Americans who understand the true legacy of our history.

When I walk around this great land, in small towns and big cities, bus stations and airports, baseball stadiums and art museums, I see an America that has expanded beyond the wildest dreams of its founders. We are a people of energy and purpose, a blended land of ever-increasing diversity that so far has proven the strength and wisdom of our great experiment. We must find a way to defeat the forces of intolerance. If we do, we will emerge a better, stronger nation.

# EXPLORATION

★ ★ ★

# Science

The legendary New York senator Daniel Patrick Moynihan famously quipped: "Everyone is entitled to his own opinion but not to his own facts." I shudder to think what the late senator would make of America today. God forbid, but if this nation ultimately fails, I believe it will be because opinions, propaganda, and superstitions replaced facts as the basis for our governance. By doing so, we will have undercut a key strength of the United States over the course of its history, one that receives too little attention: science.

When I say "science," I mean more than simply the study of biology or physics, or how much we fund basic research. Fundamentally, science is about a method of understanding our world through observation, experimentation,

and analysis. It's about allowing facts to win out over prejudice, no matter how deeply entrenched. We are seeing these
values under attack—from climate-change denial to the
questioning of our own government's statistics when they
prove to be politically inconvenient. This state of affairs is
putting the future of our nation at risk.

The United States was born in the spirit of science: What
are we, if not a great experiment? Our Founding Fathers,
shaped by the age of reason, cast aside blind faith in kings
for a bold hypothesis: Could a representative democracy
based on "certain unalienable rights" succeed? Like any scientific hypothesis, our governing philosophy has been challenged, most notably by the Civil War. (President Lincoln
called that conflict a test of whether "any nation so conceived, and so dedicated, can long endure.") But we have
kept our experiment viable by altering it through new laws
and amendments to our Constitution, just as scientific theories change to reflect new knowledge. It should come as no
surprise that many of the men who signed the Declaration of
Independence had a profound interest in science. Benjamin
Franklin was a brilliant experimentalist; Benjamin Rush
was an accomplished physician; and Thomas Jefferson had
a voracious appetite for all things science: paleontology,
astronomy, agricultural sciences, and mathematics. Some
scholars even argue that the phrasings Jefferson used in the

Declaration of Independence, especially the famous "we hold these truths to be self-evident," owe their construction to the axioms of Euclid.

As president, Jefferson would launch Meriwether Lewis and William Clark on a transcontinental expedition of discovery. Abraham Lincoln established the National Academy of Sciences. Theodore Roosevelt pioneered modern conservation. Franklin Roosevelt was the first president to appoint an official science adviser. And John F. Kennedy set the United States on the path to the moon.

A scientific approach hasn't only shaped our government; it has forged our economic might as well. In Chicago, there is a Museum of Science and Industry, and I have always felt those two disciplines go well together. We couldn't have built our mighty bridges, dams, and skyscrapers without science. And when you look at the great innovators of American history, the vast majority were men and women who believed in the benefits of testing preconceived notions through experimentation. This was the spirit that led Andrew Carnegie to revolutionize the production of steel, George Washington Carver to develop new crops, the Wright brothers to conquer flight, Henry Ford to pioneer the assembly line, and Steve Jobs to change the definition of the computer. If we are to continue as a nation of prosperity, we need to encourage this spirit of ingenuity.

But science has always had to struggle against the forces of superstition. So it would be a mistake to think that the antiscience currents we face today are entirely new. Back in 1980, the science-fiction author Isaac Asimov wrote, "There is a cult of ignorance in the United States, and there always has been. The strain of anti-intellectualism has been a constant thread winding its way through our political and cultural life, nurtured by the false notion that democracy means that 'my ignorance is just as good as your knowledge.'" It is what the comedian Stephen Colbert dubbed "truthiness," a feeling that an erroneous opinion that "sounds" true is just as valid as the actual truth. But while these forces have always been present in American society, I have never seen them infect our national discourse as much as they do now. Sadly, science has become another political football in our bifurcated United States. There was a time, not that long ago, when the Republican Party enthusiastically supported science and research. But recently many of its elected officials have embraced truthiness to guide their rhetoric and, even more damagingly, their policies. And lest we think this falls on only one side of the political divide, there is plenty of fearmongering among Democrats on issues such as genetically modified organisms.

So how did we get to a juncture in our history where we are rallying, marching, and lobbying to defend science against the forces of misinformation, greed, and narrow self-interest? There are many factors contributing to our current crisis: the political divide, a general loss of faith in experts and authority, and suspicion of corporations (such as Big Pharma and agribusiness). Science has also had some self-inflicted wounds. We have been told that chemicals like DDT were safe, we have seen unethical research like the Tuskegee Study exposed, and we are confused by shifting directives from scientists on our own health (Is fat in our diet bad or good?). In the main, these concerns are on the periphery of the vast body of scientific research, but they cannot be overlooked.

Finally—there is no kind way to say this—the press has often failed in the way we have reported on scientific findings. In many ways, television news has been the worst offender, and I do not exempt myself from this criticism. For starters, scientific issues are often complex and don't lend themselves to the simple sound bites of short news packages. We have overhyped "medical breakthroughs" that haven't been fully vetted by the scientific community, often favored the most outspoken scientific self-promoters instead of seeking out more responsible voices, and focused on gee-whiz angles instead of trying to teach the public about the important scientific principles at play.

But perhaps the biggest mistake the press makes is

falling into false equivalence. Not every scientific issue has two sides, or certainly two equal sides. And yet science "debates" are far too often reported in just such a manner. A particularly damaging example of this phenomenon can be seen in irresponsible concerns over vaccine safety. Immunizations have arguably saved more lives than any scientific advance in human history. And yet a few decades ago, charlatans—led by a now disgraced British doctor named Andrew Wakefield—started to raise fears about the general safety of vaccines. Wakefield claimed that vaccines could lead to autism, and even though his studies were highly flawed, he was given prominent press attention, including an infamous piece on *60 Minutes*. In the name of balance, Dr. Wakefield was often pitted against reputable scientists who extolled the virtues and the safety of vaccines. But when you put two people on-screen to tell both "sides" of the story, in the viewer's mind it immediately connotes fifty-fifty, even if you say it doesn't. The comedian John Oliver dramatically illustrated this point on the issue of climate change by bringing ninety-seven scientists onto the set of his HBO program to vividly demonstrate the fact that 97 percent of scientists believe human activities are leading to global warming. Needless to say, that is not how the issue has been generally covered.

There is a specialized press that covers scientific stories

with skill and nuance, and there are journalists who approach these topics thoughtfully. But in local and national newsrooms across the country, those who are tasked with covering scientific topics often emerge from the ranks of general reporters. Scientists tell me that far too often when they do engage with the press, they find that reporters oversimplify, distort, and sometimes seem bent on proving a preconceived angle. It is incumbent on journalists and storytellers to handle science better, a mission that has become a growing passion in this late chapter of my life.

I recently went to San Francisco for a meeting at the city's University of California campus (UCSF). Other schools in the state—such as UC Berkeley, UCLA, and Stanford—are far more famous. UCSF doesn't have a football team or even undergraduates, but it is one of the best science and medical research centers in the world. I toured the lab and met the students of Dr. Ron Vale, a world-renowned professor of cell biology. While still a graduate student, he discovered an ingenious chemical machine—a type of protein—that carries material around your cells by walking along specialized tracks. Vale continues to do cutting-edge research, but he also has taken on the mission of science communication with a level of passion that is inspiring. A little over a decade ago, he founded an effort aimed at democratizing science knowledge for the research community by filming seminars from famous scientists and putting them online. More recently he has become interested in expanding the scope of his program to reach a general audience, and I am trying to help him with the effort. (Full disclosure: I met Vale through my colleague Elliot Kirschner, who is working with him on these projects.)

When I visited Vale's lab, I was fascinated by how his team of thoughtful young researchers approached their work. Looking through microscopes and listening to their passionate explanations, I could grasp some of the scientific principles, but more important I could feel their enthusiasm. These women and men are explorers, as assuredly as Christopher Columbus and Neil Armstrong were. They are probing the unknown world on a microscopic level and uncovering the equivalent of new moons and continents. We may live in difficult and trying times, but these young people fill me with hope. It is our job as citizens to make sure they are supported, and my job as a journalist to effectively share their stories with the world.

I believe the public is hungry for better science reporting; it has been my experience that people of all backgrounds tend to be naturally curious and eager for knowledge about the world and their place in it. Several years ago, I did a report on neuroplasticity, the ability of our brains to keep changing even as we age. We included an interview with

Nobel Prize–winning scientist Eric Kandel, who helped pioneer the field, and his mind, keen and imaginative well into his eighties, seemed to be living proof of his discoveries. We also interviewed the Dalai Lama. It turns out His Holiness is a science enthusiast, and we learned that researchers studying Buddhist monks have discovered that their deep meditations actually alter the structure of their brains. We got a wonderful response to the program, but one viewer's email stood out. It came from a woman from Oklahoma whose job it was to work heavy construction on highway repairs. This is not the demographic that news executives think would be interested in a subtle examination of neuroplasticity, but this woman was effusive about how much she had learned. She ended her appreciative note with a phrase that has stuck with me ever since: "I always knew my mind could grow."

When I learn about scientific discoveries, I feel that my mind is growing also, but this wasn't always the case. When I was in high school, science class was an elective while woodworking and auto mechanics were required courses. At the time, this was unremarkable, the natural order of things, especially in a blue-collar neighborhood like mine. Learning about cars or carpentry was a path to good jobs. Esoteric knowledge about bacteria or the forces of physics was not perceived as a road to employment, especially for people like us. The economic needs of society were far different back then, and so too were the expectations when it came to our education.

By the time I entered college, two science courses were required for graduation, and we had our choice of chemistry, physics, biology, and botany. I took a chemistry class first, and it was not a pleasant experience. My professor was a walking stereotype who insisted on wearing a tweed jacket despite the oppressive East Texas heat in an age before air-conditioning. He was stiff and strict, and I extrapolated that science must also be a joyless pursuit. We had to memorize long lists of jargon and the entire periodic table. It might as well have been written in High Norse given my inability to understand it. Unfortunately, all this rote learning wasn't how my mind worked. I faltered, and it was one of the few Cs I got in college. When I took physics the following year, it wasn't much better. Science courses scared me, so science scared me. I was happy to leave it behind when I graduated.

The first time the importance of science really struck me was back in the early 1960s. I was working with producer David Buksbaum on the CBS News documentary investigating the tragedy of the USS *Thresher*, a nuclear submarine that was lost—with no survivors—during a deep dive exercise off the coast of Cape Cod a year earlier. I headed out to La Jolla, California, to interview celebrated oceanographer

Roger Revelle about the physics of ocean depths. From the moment I met him, I could tell I was in the presence of a world-class mind, and while I had to interview many senior navy brass for the report, no one impressed me as much as he did. He gave me a tour of his research facilities: the rows of lab benches, the unfamiliar equipment, and the tanks teeming with odd sea creatures. There was an air of exhilaration in the lab. It was a world away from my boring college science lectures. Revelle spoke humbly of the limits of our knowledge and how much of our world remained undiscovered, and suddenly it struck me: This was what science was all about. I saw a vista of exploration stretching out into the future. I left feeling more than intrigued. I was inspired.

Looking back, I now see my experience in school as a cautionary tale. I had always liked to try to figure out how things worked. And yet all that creative energy slammed into a wall of mindless memorization. I have heard many similar stories of students being turned off by science. When I recently interviewed the British Nobel Prize–winning geneticist Sir Paul Nurse, I was shocked to learn that he too had struggled in some of his introductory science classes in college. He confessed to having a terrible memory for "all the bits of information that you needed to pass exams." Like me, he also had trouble with the periodic table, but once he could make sense of the basic physics that led to the structure of the elements, then he said it all came into focus. "What really mattered for me," he explained, "was understanding the basis and the order. Then I could put the names to it. If I was just learning the names with no order, I was hopeless."

Although we have made progress, I fear that too many of our young students are getting turned off and thinking, like I did, that somehow science is not for them. Textbooks still often double as long lists of meaningless vocabulary to memorize, and the standardized tests by which we measure achievement also favor rote learning. Many scientists I have talked to bemoan the current environment. They worry that most of the lay public is unaware of the curiosity and excitement that guides the global pursuit of scientific research.

When I asked Sir Paul Nurse how to inspire young minds, he said children should do what he did when he was growing up: Head out into the night and look up at the moon and stars. "Wonder what it all means and you're already on the first step to science." The famed researcher Jennifer Doudna, a pioneer in cutting-edge gene-editing technology, told me something similar. She grew up in Hawaii spending time outdoors among all of the islands' unusual animals and simply wondering, *What makes them the way they are?*

Science is much more than the accumulation of facts; it is about the willingness to reevaluate our assumptions in the face of data to better see, understand, and improve our world. These are values that have shaped the evolution of our modern democracy, so I think science can be a bridge that helps unite us as a nation. If our elected officials turn their backs on this process, they will be undermining the forces that have elevated our country.

When you hang around scientists for a while, you are likely to hear a remarkable anecdote that looms large for them and should be a repeated lesson for the nation. The scene was 1969 on Capitol Hill at a hearing before Congress's Joint Committee on Atomic Energy. Answering questions was Robert Wilson, the director of the National Accelerator Laboratory (now called Fermilab), which was under construction in DuPage County, Illinois, just west of Chicago. The project was a particle accelerator to study seemingly abstract physics. It was a costly proposition. Dr. Wilson was questioned about the lab by Democratic senator John Pastore of Rhode Island.

SENATOR PASTORE: Is there anything connected in the hopes of this accelerator that in any way involves the security of the country?

DR. WILSON: No, sir; I do not believe so.

SENATOR PASTORE: Nothing at all?

DR. WILSON: Nothing at all.

SENATOR PASTORE: It has no value in that respect?

DR. WILSON: It only has to do with the respect with which we regard one another, the dignity of men, our love of culture. It has to do with those things. It has nothing to do with the military. I am sorry.

SENATOR PASTORE: Don't be sorry for it.

DR. WILSON: I am not, but I cannot in honesty say it has any such application.

SENATOR PASTORE: Is there anything here that projects us in a position of being competitive with the Russians, with regard to this race?

DR. WILSON: Only from a long-range point of view, of a developing technology. Otherwise, it has to do with: Are we good painters, good sculptors, great poets? I mean all the things that we really venerate and honor in our country and are patriotic about. In that sense, this new knowledge has all to do with honor and country, but it has nothing to do directly with defending our country except to help make it worth defending.

A country "worth defending"—how true. And how elegant a plea for patriotism. Science, like the arts, is about the most creative applications of the human mind. We as a species have been able to figure out so much about life and the universe—a process of discovery that is only accelerating. The fact that the United States has been a beacon for that progress should fill all Americans with pride. When the great histories of this nation are written centuries from now, I am confident that the role of science will occupy many chapters. I desperately hope we can keep that narrative going, and even growing. Our country's future place in the world depends on that.

# Books

D anny, show them your library card."

I was a young boy, on my first journey downtown to the main branch of the Houston Public Library. It was the most spectacular building I had ever seen. And I was being told I had a special key—a library card—that could unlock all the knowledge that surrounded me: the thousands of titles printed in the card catalog, the stacks that seemed to go on for miles. I, the son of an oil field worker, now belonged here among the books. I dug in my pocket and produced my prized possession.

This experience was not unique. In small farming towns and big industrial cities, in immigrant neighborhoods and in wealthy communities, young children and people of all ages could, and did, head to libraries in large numbers to access a world of knowledge for free. Hundreds of libraries across the nation, often among the most beautiful buildings in their communities, had been built over the late-nineteenth and early-twentieth centuries through the largesse of the industrialist Andrew Carnegie. As a young man, Carnegie hadn't been able to afford a fee to a private library, and it was an experience he never forgot. He believed there should be no barriers to books and study, that knowledge should be democratic. As with so much of the American story, a glaring exception to this narrative centered on race. Most libraries in the South—including Houston—were segregated, and some Carnegie funds were set aside for "colored" libraries.

I recognize a quaintness in waxing nostalgic about libraries in an age when we have instantaneous access to more information than was contained in all the combined library collections of my youth. Still, libraries represent an aspirational notion of democracy. They were, and still are, civic institutions that welcome anyone who wishes to become a more informed and independent citizen. In books we can find expert and trustworthy scholarship on any subject imaginable. By reading books, we can continually challenge our own biases and learn beyond our level of formal education. These are qualities that are needed now more than ever.

Historically, leaders across the political spectrum have encouraged a reverence for knowledge. There was a belief that our civic discourse should be infused with informed and well-reasoned arguments. This has been a fundamental cornerstone of our democracy, stretching back to the birth of the United States. Just as we have statues and memorials to great battles and political leaders, we have monuments to knowledge. Perhaps one of the most elegant examples is the Dome Room in the Rotunda at the University of Virginia. If you stand in the center and look in all directions, you will see columns framing magnificent windows with sweeping views. Hidden from your sight line, in an ingenious piece of architectural design, are grand bookshelves radiating out toward the windows like spokes in a great wheel of learning. The expanse of the beautiful Virginia landscape is what is visible, but the words, the scholarship, and the books, though invisible in the moment, are what give the space its meaning. This room, the building that houses it, and the University of Virginia itself were the creation of Thomas Jefferson, who embodied the contradictions into which our nation was born. He loved learning and reason and wrote eloquent pleas for freedom and enlightenment in our Declaration of Independence. But in a spectacular example of human frailty, he failed to extend his grand notions of the brotherhood of the human race to men, women, and children in bondage—including those he owned and the mother of his unacknowledged children.

Jefferson's beloved library reminds us that reason and knowledge are necessary but ultimately insufficient for a moral government. On the one hand, words have power—the power to declare independence, establish a government, and draft a bill of rights. But since words are interpreted by imperfect men and women, the history of this republic is full of countless examples of those in power failing to live up to the spirit of "all men are created equal."

However, it would be a mistake to see only hypocrisy in the University of Virginia's library. The building's very structure reflects how the young United States fundamentally differed from Old Europe. Jefferson modeled his Rotunda after the Pantheon in Rome, but whereas the original was built as a temple to the gods, Jefferson created his as a place for scholarship. And although most universities in Jefferson's time also viewed the teaching of religion as a core mission, with a church occupying a place of prominence on campus, Jefferson felt differently. Instead of a church, he built his library.

The term "temple of learning" is often used today as a metaphor, but that is literally what Jefferson conceived of for his library. The grand cathedrals of Europe, with their soaring ceilings, stained glass, and evocative statuary, were designed to strike awe into the hearts of the common people, who spent most of their hard lives in squalor. Jefferson understood that a beautifully designed library could encourage reverence for the type of scholarship that he and so many other Founding Fathers believed was vital for building a republic.

If you travel to Washington, D.C., you can see our country's debt to the power of books in the very heart of our federal city. Next to the Supreme Court and facing the great dome of the Capitol is the Library of Congress. I find the symbolism inspiring: three institutions that write, judge, and archive the words and thoughts that allow our nation to function. The Library of Congress was founded in 1800 with a modest mission, a reference resource for Congress. But that changed after the British burned Washington during the War of 1812 and the original collection was lost. In response, Thomas Jefferson offered to sell his own library to the U.S. government. His collection of books was considered one of the finest in the New World, containing thousands of volumes on almost every topic imaginable—not just law, statecraft, and history, but also the sciences, philosophy, and the arts. To those who argued that such a disparate set of works was unnecessary for a Library of Congress, Jefferson responded, "There is in fact no subject to which a member of Congress may not have occasion to refer."

The library now had a bold new direction—a reservoir for capturing the world's knowledge. This mission was enhanced greatly in 1870, when Congress stipulated that the library must receive two copies of every book, map, photograph, or other such work that was submitted for copyright in the United States. This caused the collection to expand exponentially, and the pace of growth continues at what is now the largest library in the world. The building on Capitol Hill—with a domed ceiling soaring 160 feet above its spectacular reading room—is itself a beautiful temple of learning. A guidebook from around the time the new building opened in 1897 celebrated Jefferson's idea of an expansive collection and perfectly captures my feelings for this singular institution. "America is justly proud of this gorgeous and palatial monument to its National sympathy and appreciation of Literature, Science, and Art. It has been designed and executed entirely by American art and American labor [and is] a fitting tribute for the great thoughts of generations past, present, and to be."

Growing up in a working-class Houston, I had never heard of the Library of Congress or the grand Rotunda at the University of Virginia, but my local branch of the Houston Public Library showed me that books were not only important, they were also objects of beauty. The stone building had high ceilings, big windows, and a red tile roof; its Italian-style architecture made the library seem worlds away from my hardscrabble neighborhood. I was pleased that it later became a recognized historic landmark. Even as a high school student, I would often prolong my walk home from school to go by the library. It may sound sappy, but the building inspired me to dream of exploring a world greater than the one I knew.

But while the library's physical charm was impressive, it was what was inside that made it truly magical. I was a voracious reader and spent countless hours in what became a sort of second home. I was following, in my own small way, the path laid out by Jefferson, Carnegie, and all the others who believed in the power of books. And I had a wonderful guide, the librarian Jimmie May Hicks, who served at the Heights branch library from the year of my birth, 1931, until her death in 1964—more than three decades of quiet but consequential service to her community and nation. Like all the best librarians, Ms. Hicks would suggest, question, and prod my reading into new and unexpected directions. The library now has a memorial plaque in her honor that reads, in part, *She dedicated her life to her profession and sought always to impart to others joy in acquiring knowledge and pleasure in the art of reading.* She was a true patriot.

The importance of curated knowledge was encouraged at home as well. During my last year of elementary school, our principal called in all the parents to prepare them for the challenges of junior high. She talked about not only the looming physical changes of adolescence but also the mental growth that would be required for us to thrive in a more rigorous and less protective academic environment. My mother was a good listener, and she came back determined that what the Rather household needed now more than anything was our own set of encyclopedias. This caused a bit of a disagreement with my father, who insisted this was a luxury we couldn't afford. But my mother insisted that if we bought them on an installment plan, we could make it work. Ultimately, she prevailed with the winning argument that "just having them in the house will help Danny" (and my younger brother, Don, and sister, Patricia).

When boxes packed with the many volumes of the *World Book Encyclopedia* arrived at our doorstep, it was a momentous day. If memory serves me correctly, we had the choice of ordering the set with either red or blue on the spines and my mother chose red because she felt it would stand out more on the shelves. The books were wonderfully bound and you could feel the weight of knowledge simply by opening them in your lap and flipping through the pages. My mother was right; just having those books on our shelves transformed our home. Whenever any of us had a question, there was the promise of an answer, and an excuse for more learning. My father's initial reluctance dissipated and I can still see him rising from reading the newspaper, walking deliberately to the shelf, and pulling out the right alphabetical volume to look up a name, location, or concept. I kept that encyclopedia set well into my thirties.

We need to continue to teach our children how to read, not just to sound out words, but also to read deeply and thoroughly. This must start early with the understanding that books are important. I interviewed the music legend Dolly Parton a few years back, and her naturally effervescent personality really sparkled when we started talking about books. Parton had grown up in the poverty of Appalachia. She told me about her father, a smart man who had to drop out of school at a young age to work to support his family. He never learned to read properly. With him in mind, Parton founded a charity in 1995 to provide books to families in her home county of Sevier, Tennessee. The idea was simple: Families would receive age-appropriate books every month from when a child was born up until he or she turned five. The program has grown considerably, first to communities across the state, then the United States, and now to countries overseas. Today, more than one million children are enrolled and over eighty million books have been shipped. As Parton told me, "If you can read, you can educate yourself. That was my main point." By teaching children to educate themselves, Parton and others like her are helping to renew the same democratic spirit that I had discovered at my local library.

But I can think of no better summation of the importance of books to our democracy than the story of Frederick Douglass. In his masterful 1845 autobiography, *Narrative of the Life of Frederick Douglass, an American Slave*, Douglass opened many people's eyes to the horrors of slavery. It wasn't just the dramatic arc of his life; it was the beauty with which he wrote it, and it was also who was doing the writing. The book's frontispiece proclaimed that the narrative was "WRITTEN BY HIMSELF." How could a man write so insightfully and be held in bondage to another? Many reviewers at the time noted this fact. Margaret Fuller, writing in the *New-York Daily Tribune*, stated, "Considered merely as a narrative, we have never read one more simple, true, coherent, and warm with genuine feeling. It is an excellent piece of writing, and on that score to be prized as a specimen of the powers of the Black Race, which Prejudice persists in disputing. We prize highly all evidence of this kind, and it is becoming more abundant."

Books and literacy are central to Douglass's *Narrative*, particularly the story of how he learned to read at the age of twelve while living in Baltimore. His master's wife had taught him the alphabet, and Douglass became eager for much more. He started exchanging food for reading lessons from the poor white boys in the neighborhood. "This bread I used to bestow on the hungry little urchins, who, in return, would give me the more valuable bread of knowledge." Douglass devoured the books he could get his hands on, but his self-education was a bittersweet exercise. "I would at times feel that learning to read had been a curse rather than a blessing. It had given me a view of my wretched condition, without the remedy. It opened my eyes to the horrible pit, but to no ladder upon which to get out. In moments of agony, I envied my fellow-slaves for their stupidity." Douglass would eventually escape to the North and help change the fate of millions of enslaved human beings through the power of his words.

Today Douglass's papers are in the Library of Congress, the collection started by the slaveholding Thomas Jefferson. It strikes me as an act of poetic justice and a symbol of how the breadth of ideas we consider vital for our national identity has expanded. We could not have made this journey without scholarship and thought, debate and self-reflection. To be sure, words are not enough on their own. For all of Douglass's eloquence and moral certitude, for example, abolition required a civil war. And social justice movements have required acts of protest and demonstration. But what I learned as a young child, and it's a lesson I have seen repeated countless times, is that a democracy requires open access to ideas. It requires a willingness to struggle and learn, to question our own suppositions and biases, to open ourselves as citizens, and a nation, to a world of books and thought. If we become a country of superficiality and easy answers based on assumptions and not one steeped in reason and critical learning, we will have lost the foundation of our founding and all that has allowed our nation to grow into our modern United States. Progress cannot be only intuited. It must be written, and read.

We find ourselves in a singular moment in our nation's history, where we have political leaders openly scornful of intellectualism and scholarship. Our civic norms are being trampled and academic independence is under threat. From our health care debate to our economic policy and questions about climate change, we see many in power denigrate expertise and freely make up their own "facts" to fit their theories. So much of our public policy seems to follow a mantra of "Go with your gut." It doesn't matter what the details are, as long as you are winning, and a perverse calculus has gripped Washington wherein reckless sloganeering and obstruction has replaced governing by consultation, debate, and consensus. This scorn of knowledge (especially when the conclusions are painful) in exchange for fact-free rhetoric is not entirely new in our history, but it has always been the language of demagoguery and it is a betrayal of our traditions.

Our nation was born in a spirit of fierce debate. Our Founding Fathers had sharp political differences, but they were almost all deep readers, writers, and thinkers. When they set about to create a modern republic, they went into their libraries and pulled out the works of philosophers such as John Locke and Thomas Hobbes. They consulted the Greeks, the Romans, the philosophers of Europe, and the Bible. They revered the power of the written word and how it enabled a nation free from the whims of a king. As John Adams wrote, a republic "is a government of laws, and not of men." A government of laws is a government of reason, and a government of books. That was true at our founding, and we must ensure that it remains a hallmark of our future.

# The Arts

These days it is easier to occupy young minds with mobile phones and tablet computers, but I have a special respect for the mothers and fathers who continue to lug around the bags of crayons, markers, and paper. It brings a smile to my face when I see a child drawing. And while I know there are museum- and concertgoers who are irritated by sharing the spaces with sometimes unruly children, I am encouraged when I see generations of the future engaging with the arts. These pursuits are central to our American identity. Patriotism can burst to the surface through many geysers of expression.

Perhaps one of the most inspiring visions for our nation can be found in a letter John Adams wrote to his wife,

Abigail. It was the spring of 1780, he was serving a diplomatic post in Paris, and the final outcome of the Revolutionary War was still in doubt. But Adams had his eyes firmly set on the future. "I must study Politicks and War that my sons may have liberty to study Mathematicks and Philosophy . . . in order to give their Children a right to study Painting, Poetry, [and] Musick." It's an incredibly hopeful articulation of progress whereby the lasting worth of a nascent nation would depend on the arts being cultivated, encouraged, and appreciated. But there is another important current running through Adams's letter, a notion that American art would have to await future generations. This sense of cultural inferiority would stretch well past the colonial era.

My first introduction to what might be considered art (at the time narrowly defined as high culture) came in high school. But we weren't taught to celebrate the power of free expression in a vibrant American democracy. Instead, art was described to us mainly as a product of Old World refinement and a necessary accoutrement for those of us intent on climbing the social ladder. We were brought to the symphony, the art museum, the ballet, and the theater, but the impact was largely lost on us. Eventually I came to enjoy all the art forms that hadn't impressed me as a teenager, but it took time and exposure. I now realize that my early lack of interest was also born from fear. I believed that understanding art was beyond my capabilities. It was as if I had internalized the cultural insecurities of the United States.

This way of thinking was common in mid-twentieth-century America. Although the United States had just rescued Europe from the conflagration of fascism, we still had a profound inferiority complex when it came to assessing our own cultural value. Every city wanted a museum of fine arts (collections of mostly European paintings and sculptures) and a symphony conducted by a European maestro. Even NBC had its own orchestra led by the acclaimed Italian conductor Arturo Toscanini. In postwar Houston, pretension outstripped our modest reality. We wanted to imagine ourselves as a great American city, and the community leaders saw the arts as paramount to achieving status. Legend has it that the Houston Symphony approached the wealthy oilman Robert Everett Smith (everyone called him "Ree Bob") to raise money to bring the famous conductor Leopold Stokowski to the city. According to the story, when Ree Bob was told they needed $1 million and had him down for half, he replied that he would give the entire amount if he didn't have to actually go hear the orchestra in person. Whether true or a tall tale, this story nevertheless captured the mood of the times. For many Americans, especially the ones I knew growing up, art felt elitist and far removed from our daily blue-collar lives. Luckily for me, in more ways than one, that was about to change.

When I met Jean, we were in our early twenties and she had an enthusiastic thirst for the arts. She loved to paint and go to art exhibits. I wanted to impress her, so on our second date I took her to the Alley Theatre, which has since become one of Houston's most cherished institutions. The Alley was the brainchild of Nina Vance, who gained a national reputation for proving that a town like Houston could handle serious works for the stage. The play Jean and I saw that night was *The Glass Menagerie* by Tennessee Williams. I was transfixed by the production onstage, and by my date sitting next to me. I knew I wanted to accompany Jean on a lifetime of performances, and over our six decades of marriage, we have done that.

Through Jean, whose education began, literally, in a one-room schoolhouse in rural Texas, I learned to appreciate art, symphonic music, and opera. When we relocated to the cultural mecca of New York, we witnessed the rise and fall of artistic fads and saw the first big shows of artists who went on to become household names. I also started to see art as an increasingly democratic enterprise. I came to realize that the masterful lyrics of Hank Williams's "I'm So Lonesome I Could Cry" were much more than just a radio ballad; they were American poetry: "The silence of a falling star lights up a purple sky." Similarly, the best Broadway shows, like *Oklahoma!*, and Hollywood films, like *Citizen Kane*, were not simply entertainment but uniquely American art forms. And jazz like Duke Ellington's "Take the A Train" demanded the same seriousness as a Beethoven symphony. As I started to take all this in, I appreciated that art shouldn't be about impressing others; whether you are an individual or a nation, art is about engaging in a candid dialogue with yourself.

We now understand that the great American story is not confined to history books or political speeches. It is sung, and danced, and dramatized, and turned into verse. It is painted, and sculpted, and written, and filmed. Artists may not swear an oath to serve in government or the military, but they swear an oath to freedom of expression that is no less worthy of recognition, especially in a democracy such as ours. Theirs are not always comfortable voices to hear, or even comfortable people to be around. But they are the truth tellers whose works have challenged our national complacency, like Woody Guthrie's songs; held up mirrors to the darker corners of our society, as do the photographs of Jacob Riis; and summoned the winds of justice, like the novels of Toni Morrison. American artists have also taken the grand artistic traditions of the rest of the world and unapologetically created something dynamic and new, such as my fellow Texan the choreographer Alvin Ailey. He married the forms of classical ballet with the deep spiritual and musical traditions of the African American community to worldwide acclaim.

Our art has been, like our country, boisterous and courageous and gloriously distinct. It has expressed euphoria, shame, and outrage. It has been exalted and it has felt the sting of suppression and marginalization. It has been misunderstood. Perhaps most important, our art has been wonderfully diverse. Our corporate boardrooms do not represent America; neither does our Congress, Supreme Court, nor certainly those we have elected to the presidency. But our artistic community represents the United States in all its multiple wonders.

Any list of great American artists would be woefully incomplete if it did not celebrate the broad democratic stirrings of a diverse nation. Consider one idiosyncratic sampling: Louis Armstrong and Mark Twain and Martha Graham, Emily Dickinson and Ella Fitzgerald and Edward Hopper, William Faulkner and Andy Warhol and Bob Dylan, Langston Hughes and Jackson Pollock and Charlie Chaplin, Johnny Cash and Georgia O'Keeffe and Frank Lloyd Wright, Miles Davis and Willa Cather and Ansel Adams, Willie Nelson and Maya Angelou and Martin Scorsese, George Gershwin and Marlon Brando and Prince, Elvis

Presley and Carlos Santana and Stephen Sondheim, Maria Tallchief and Robin Williams and Ernest Hemingway. The list could go on and on. American art is proof that people from all backgrounds and corners of this country have something important to say.

Back in 1982, we ended a *CBS Evening News* broadcast with a profile of a quirky artist who was making impromptu line drawings in chalk around New York City. It was one of those slice-of-life pieces—the humorous and heartwarming stories that we use to round out the more serious news of the day. I set it up with a bit of humor: "One subway artist is making a name for himself somewhere besides the police blotter." The artist was indeed starting to make a name for himself, and he became one of our more famous pop artists. His name was Keith Haring, and he was just a kid from Kutztown, Pennsylvania, who felt that art should be accessible to everyone. Sadly, we lost him at age thirty-one, a life, like so many others, cut short by AIDS. But his unique voice continues to speak to us. That is the wonder of the immortality of art.

Our Founding Fathers understood that free expression was central to democracy, a core value that separates us from autocratic and despotic societies where artists are often targeted as subversive and dangerous. In the spring of 2011, we were working on a report about government censorship in China when we interviewed one of the country's most famous contemporary artists, Ai Weiwei. Ai had already been the subject of harassments and even severe beatings at the hands of government authorities who were not pleased by his art. He had become a fierce critic of the corruption that led to shoddily built schools that had collapsed during a major earthquake in 2008. Thousands of young students had been crushed to death. In one work, Ai laid out nine thousand colorful children's backpacks to spell out "For seven years she lived happily on this earth," a eulogy from a mother of one of the victims. It was a stark message, amplified by the urgency of the artwork. And it was not the kind of message Chinese authorities liked to hear.

Just ten days after our interview, Ai was arrested, and he was held for eighty-one days without charges. His work is now suppressed in his home country. "The harm of a censorship system is not just that it impoverishes intellectual life," Ai wrote in a column for the *New York Times* in 2017. "It also fundamentally distorts the rational order in which the natural and spiritual worlds are understood. The censorship system relies on robbing a person of the self-perception that one needs in order to maintain an independent existence. It cuts off one's access to independence and happiness."

The idea of art as "access to independence and happiness" is a notion that speaks to my own experience. In art, you can find voices that channel your own life story better than you could ever express it yourself. And you can also find voices that introduce you to worlds you would never have otherwise visited. In a diverse republic such as ours, both of these inspirations are especially important.

One American artist whose work spoke to me with uncanny resonance was the greatly underappreciated playwright Horton Foote. He and I both were born in the same small Texas town of Wharton (although I moved to Houston when I was a year old), and we came to know each other after finding our ways to New York much later in life. Foote is perhaps best known for his Academy Award–winning screenplay for the 1962 film adaptation of *To Kill a Mockingbird*, and he was considered a skilled dramatizer of the works of Southern literature (William Faulkner was particularly pleased with Foote's adaptations of his stories). But it is Foote's original work that stands out to me as a mark of greatness. Foote's plays, screenplays, and memoirs are centered on an America that once was the norm but now has largely disappeared: small-town, rural life where families intersected with one another countless times across the generations. His work beats with the heart of a democratic nation, as he transformed the drama and comedy of everyday life into great art through his exquisite sense of dialogue. His Academy Award–winning films *Tender Mercies*, about a country music singer seeking redemption, and *The Trip to Bountiful*, about an old woman returning one last time to the farmland of her youth, echo an America in social, cultural, and geographic transformation. And they remind me that some of the best art is the most modest in its framing and far reaching in its emotional impact.

Foote's America is one that I knew well. His characters act and talk like the family, friends, and neighbors of my youth. But the rapturous reviews he received and the awards he was given, like the Pulitzer Prize for drama, are proof that he was able to capture the common nobility of our nation. I hope that Horton Foote's work will continue to be shown for as long as there is American theater, but I worry that his deceptively simple and superficially dated plays are perhaps falling out of favor. In art, as in our country more broadly, we cannot allow only the newest, loudest, and brashest voices to be heard.

While Foote always felt familiar, art also has a way of exposing you to a point of view you never could have imagined. That is the case with one of my favorite singers— and, more important, songwriters: the country star Loretta Lynn. A coal miner's daughter who rose from poverty-stricken Appalachia to Nashville royalty, she epitomized the Horatio Alger stories and the American Dream, albeit with a very important twist. Loretta Lynn achieved all this as a female artist. Lynn's catalog of songs is one of the most impressive collections of socially relevant commentary in the history of American music. As early as 1966, she was challenging her audience with a mournful story of a woman losing her husband to the Vietnam War. Entitled "Dear Uncle Sam," it included poignant lyrics such as, "You said you really need him, but you don't need him like I do." Lynn painted the lives of working-class women with honesty and humor. And she was undeterred in the face of opposition. She once told me, about her songs being banned, "When they don't play 'em, you know it's gonna be a hit." Many radio stations at the time refused to play "The Pill," a funny and yet fierce ode to women's empowerment (which Lynn recorded but didn't write). Released in 1975, it became her top crossover hit on the pop charts. I don't think anybody had heard anything like it, with lines like, "You've set this chicken your last time, 'cause now I've got the pill."

Lynn brought the intimate experiences of working-class American women to the nation's airwaves, whether it was about a girl losing her virginity in "Wings Upon Your Horns," the stigma of divorce on women in "Rated X" ("Divorce is the key to bein' loose and free, so you're gonna be talked about"), or the struggles of marriage in "Don't Come Home a Drinkin'" ("No, don't come home a drinkin' with lovin' on your mind, just stay out there on the town and see what you can find"). The rock star Jack White told me once that he revered Lynn's work: "It was the female side of our species speaking, finally, for themselves out loud." And Lynn told me herself, "When I'd go to do a show, all the women would be out there. 'I'm with you,' you know? And they'd holler at me and say, 'You come to talk to us women.'" A lot of men also learned something from her songs, this one included. I consider her another patriotic artist, a fearless social commentator channeling the experiences of an overlooked segment of society.

As I have traveled to countless museums over the years with Jean, I have been struck by how transformative art can be, and few exhibitions have moved me more than a 2015 showing of Jacob Lawrence's iconic series of sixty tempera paintings at the Museum of Modern Art in New York. Produced over the course of 1940 and 1941, the series tells one of the truly epochal transformations of the American experience: the exodus of millions of African Americans from the rural, agricultural South to the urban, industrial North and Midwest. Initially called *The Migration of the Negro*, the series was renamed by Lawrence to *The Migration Series* a few years before his death in 2000. It tells a cautionary tale of persecution and discrimination—in the South and the North. Its power lies in Lawrence's ability to distill these experiences down to a starkly beautiful or brutal image. Each picture in the series is a complete drama and part of the bigger whole. And they are paired with simple but evocative captions, like one painting of huddled black faces wrapped in colorful blankets and seated in rows of bench seats with the corresponding text: "The trains were packed continually with migrants." The review of the show in the *New York Times* does a better job than I can to explain the spell cast by the works: "[E]ven from a distance, standing in the middle of the room, you can pick up the formal links and syncopations. Dark, dense compositions alternate with open, light ones. Geometric dominance—vertical, horizontal, diagonal—shifts from panel to panel. Single rich colors—rust-pink, mustard, sherbet-green—recur, threading through the whole like the sound of bright instruments in an orchestra." The paintings are a brilliant evocation of an entire historical movement, provocative and emotionally distilled in a way that is achievable only through art.

Lawrence was twenty-three years old when he finished the series, and he painted all sixty pieces at the same time to give them a unified feel. When they debuted at a gallery in Manhattan, it marked the first such showing for an African American artist. The curatorial materials that accompanied the recent MoMA show explained that Lawrence researched the migration in great detail. However, he also tapped into a world of artistic expression much bigger than his own voice. Lawrence was living in New York in the midst of the great flowering of African American culture of the Harlem Renaissance, and one need not be a scholar to see the crosscurrents of influences in the work. The exhibition placed Lawrence's series alongside documentary photographs and journalism that had inspired him. There was film of the great Marian Anderson singing "My Country, 'Tis of Thee" on the steps of the Lincoln Memorial in 1939 after she had been banned from singing at Constitution Hall by the Daughters of the American Revolution. (It was Eleanor Roosevelt who helped change the venue of the concert.) Anderson's beautiful operatic voice, breaking through stifling racial barriers, is a potent symbol of the incongruities inherent in American art.

For me, the most effective accompaniment to Lawrence's work in the show was film of Billie Holiday singing "Strange Fruit," the chilling song about lynching.

> Southern trees bear strange fruit
> Blood on the leaves and blood at the root
> Black bodies swinging in the southern breeze
> Strange fruit hanging from the poplar trees

The word "lynching" is never mentioned in the song, but the terror and horror of the act is palpable. Similarly,

Lawrence addresses lynching in a pair of paintings in his series, but neither shows a dead body. In the first, we see a living figure sitting huddled in terror or sadness beneath a noose on a leafless branch. The text accompanying the images is all the more searing for its simplicity: "Another cause [of the migration] was lynching. It was found that where there had been a lynching, the people who were reluctant to leave at first left immediately after this." In the second, we see a female figure sitting at a stark wooden table with her head in her arms in sorrow.

Taking in Lawrence's paintings and the song "Strange Fruit," I was struck by the power of art to move me. As a young reporter, I had witnessed the lethal results of institutionalized racism firsthand, and standing there in the bright galleries of the MoMA, I was transported back across time and distance. I wasn't just thinking. I was feeling.

I was curious about the story behind "Strange Fruit," and I was in for a surprise. It was written by Abel Meeropol, a child of Jewish immigrants who taught at a public high school in the Bronx. He had seen a photograph of a lynching victim that he couldn't get out of his mind, and he turned that into a poem, and then put it to music. The song eventually found its way to Holiday, who made it into a classic. (In 1999, *Time* magazine dubbed it the song of the century.)

Art is an attempt to capture the truths of the world as

you see it in a medium you can share with others. It is about lending your voice, your perspective to local, national, and global conversations. And that is why, in the United States in particular, our definition of what is art and who is an artist must be as varied as our citizenry.

I am relieved that we have escaped the narrow definitions of art from my childhood, a development gloriously celebrated in the musical *Hamilton*. Lin-Manuel Miranda, the creative genius behind the show, has tapped into the broadest currents of America's modern musical traditions and made the case that they are important and profound. He has captured the attention of young and old alike, and people from across the political spectrum, with a story that is rooted in the awe-inspiring heterogeneity of America. This work of art has brought people together and inspired them to look with fresh eyes on our common history. Schoolchildren now listen to the soundtrack and see themselves in the multitude of voices. It is testimony to the sheer power of the piece that it all seems so apparent and obvious in retrospect, that you can tell a story of a Founding Father using hip-hop and other such urgent new forms of expression. Sadly, the incredible success of *Hamilton* means that ticket prices in New York and in its traveling shows are out of reach for most Americans. We must find creative ways to ensure that great art like this is accessible to not only the rich and well connected, but to everyone.

Our art is our story. It grows with the inclusion of different peoples and cultures, and we are stronger for it. Watching *Hamilton*, I remembered how in a previous era those who pioneered the musical traditions that Miranda was exalting were not really considered artists by the cultural elites. And there was a time, not so long ago, when these young, beautiful, diverse actors and musicians would be told that their voices were not worthy of inclusion on Broadway stages or in concert halls. What *Hamilton* shows so brilliantly through its modern, vibrant musical score is that this spirit of innovation and experimentation in art echoes the narrative of the founding of our nation. It is the ultimate story of freedom. And it is a vital part of what unites us.

# RESPONSIBILITY

# The Environment

There is an image you've probably seen of a bright marble set against complete blackness. The marble sits in a shadow. It is mostly blue and swirling white, with a hint of green and brown. In the foreground of the photograph is a swath of barren gray. This picture is considered one of the most iconic images in human history. It altered our sense of ourselves as a species and the place we call home, because that marble is our planet seen from the vastness of space, and the gray horizon we see in the foreground is the moon. The photograph has a name: *Earthrise*.

The image was captured by astronaut William Anders of *Apollo 8* on the first manned mission to orbit the lunar sphere, and the photograph can be seen as a mirror image for every vision humans had ever experienced up to that point. From before the dawn of history, our ancestors looked up in the night sky and saw a brilliant moon, often in shadow. But in that moment on *Apollo 8*, three men from our planet looked back and saw all the rest of us on a small disk with oceans, clouds, and continents.

This image, so peaceful and yet so breathtaking, was taken at the end of a turbulent year. It was Christmas Eve 1968, but from up there you would never know that a hot war was raging in Vietnam or that a Cold War was dividing Europe. You wouldn't know of the assassinations of Dr. Martin Luther King Jr. or Bobby Kennedy. From that distance, people are invisible, and so are cities, countries, and national boundaries. All that separates us ethnically, culturally, politically, and spiritually is absent from the image. What we see is one fragile planet making its way across the vastness of space.

There was something about that photograph that struck deep into the souls of many people about our place in the heavens, and a year later it appeared on a postage stamp (six cents at the time) with the caption "In the beginning God . . ." The photograph is also widely credited with galvanizing a movement to protect our planet. Over the course of the 1960s, people increasingly spoke of a Spaceship Earth, a notion eloquently voiced by United States ambassador Adlai Stevenson in a speech he gave to the United Nations in 1965. "We travel together, passengers on a little space ship, dependent on its vulnerable reserves of air and soil; all committed for our safety to its security and peace; preserved from annihilation only by the care, the work, and, I will say, the love we give our fragile craft." With the *Earthrise* photograph, suddenly Spaceship Earth was no longer a metaphor. It was there for all of us to see.

The 1960s and 1970s were times of such social upheaval that the environmental movement is often overlooked. But real action was happening. In 1962, Rachel Carson, a trained marine biologist, published one of the most important books in American history, *Silent Spring*. It focused on the dangers of synthetic pesticides like DDT, showing how these chemicals could insidiously enter an ecosystem and wreak unintended havoc on the health of a wide range of animals, including humans. The book hit like a thunderclap. The reaction from the chemical industry was fierce and unrelenting, but the public uproar was even more substantial.

The moral weight of Carson's argument changed the equation for how we measured our actions; the health of the earth became part of the discussion. That book contributed to the rising pressure on government officials to act to protect our planet, and in 1970 we saw both the founding of the Environmental Protection Agency (signed into law by President Richard Nixon) and the first Earth Day (organized by Wisconsin's Democratic senator Gaylord Nelson). The year also saw an important expansion of the Clean Air Act (first passed in 1963). The Clean Water Act would come in 1972. The environment was now an important national priority, and support for it was bipartisan.

For all the talk of Spaceship Earth and Earth Day, however, there was a belief at the time that environmentalism was a series of local battles. When it came to air and water pollution, we worried about the health of the smog over Los Angeles and the chemical runoff into the Hudson River. Over time, we saw environmental threats become more regional, with acid rain and the depletion of the ozone layer. It was hard to imagine, though, that we could harm the planet on a global scale. But all the while, ever since the start of the industrial revolution, an odorless and invisible pollutant was being pumped into our atmosphere with increasing volume—from our tailpipes, smokestacks, and the clear-cutting of forests. We now know that carbon dioxide and the resulting climate change is a threat of a magnitude unlike anything we have ever seen before. Those are the stakes we face today.

In the summer of 2007, I traveled 450 miles north of the Arctic Circle to the Canadian tundra to report on a development that was shocking for any student of history. For centuries, famed explorers had searched for a shipping route from Europe to Asia through the frigid north. It was dubbed the Northwest Passage, and it proved to be a deadly and illusory dream, as many ships and men went in to never return. So when my colleagues and I heard reports that melting sea ice was possibly unlocking the passage, we set about to document the dramatic climate change at the end of the earth. Some of my crew spent days aboard a Canadian Coast Guard research icebreaker, and I met them in the Inuit village of Arctic Bay, population about 700 hardy souls.

What both the scientists and the local inhabitants understood was that a world of ice was undergoing rapid and unpredictable change. I remember taking a walk along a rocky shoreline with an elderly Inuit woman, who pointed at the open water and explained how, even in the summer, it had once been largely ice. She talked of seal pelts that were not as thick because of the warmer water and her worries that her people's way of life was in danger of being irrevocably lost. Meanwhile, on the research boat, scientists were rushing to understand how this changing climate was affecting marine life and whether they could find clues to the arctic environment of the past by dredging the bottom of the sea.

It is an awesome realization that Earth, which has always seemed boundless, is so susceptible to the negative byproducts of human activity. Perhaps that is what makes it difficult for some to accept climate change. As we walk through nature, it seems so robust and permanent. And for the vast majority of the history of our species, we did not have the power to destroy the planet.

But if you look back to the beginning of the environmental movement, you will see that it sprang from a dawning realization of how damaging humans could be. In the late nineteenth century, the mighty bison of the American West, estimated to once have numbered in the tens of millions, were slaughtered over just a few decades to the brink of extinction. Hunting parties would shoot indiscriminately from train windows as sport, leaving thousands of carcasses to rot in the sun. A seemingly limitless resource suddenly was on the verge of disappearing. By then, a growing spirit of naturalism was capturing the nation's attention, personified by writers like Henry David Thoreau. And leading citizens in the United States, men with political power like Theodore Roosevelt, decided to act.

They formed conservation clubs that began to have an effect on the federal government. Yellowstone National Park, considered the first national park in the world, was founded in 1872. Yosemite was added in 1890. A movement had been born. But meanwhile, a very different revolution had begun half a world away. The first modern internal combustion engine was built in the 1870s, and in

1886 German engineer Karl Benz patented the first motor-car. Over the ensuing century and decades, as the environmental movement grew in its scope and importance, Earth was getting sicker.

None of this was known when I was growing up. The Texas economy of my youth was literally being fueled by oil, and there seemed to be nothing incompatible with black gold and the health of the wide world outside my door. Some of my earliest memories were of running through the wild meadow that bordered my neighborhood on the outskirts of Houston, looking at bugs, lizards, and, it being Texas, a lot of snakes. There was a creek a little farther out, and when I was young, my mother made it known to me that it was a boundary I dare not cross. Beyond the creek lay deep woods, and as I grew older, I was allowed to wander alone beneath the strong oaks and towering pines, turned loose in nature. In the midst of the woods was the Buffalo Bayou, and I learned how to swim in its languid waters. In truth, the bayou had already been polluted by the oil refineries and chemical plants around Houston. But we boys, frolicking in the water, didn't know that. We were living out our fantasies of being latter-day Tom Sawyers and Huck Finns.

In that great meadow and the forest beyond, the world seemed exciting and alive. It was teeming with rabbits, squirrels, and the occasional coyote. There were birds in the skies and all those snakes on the ground. Most were harmless, but there were poisonous ones as well—rattlesnakes, water moccasins, coral snakes, and the spreading adder, what we called the "spreadin' adder." My mother worried about snakes, but she knew that they were part of the Lone Star way of life. You had to be alert, knowledgeable, careful, and a bit lucky—just like in life.

My father was the kind of hunter who believed that you shouldn't hunt something you don't know a lot about, and he instilled in me a deep respect for the natural world. As we walked together on warm summer evenings, his hunting rifle in hand, he would explain the life cycle of rabbits and that the best place to find squirrels was where the "hardwoods met the pine trees," because squirrels liked the height of the pine trees and the nuts of the hardwoods. Whether this was provable from scientific study, or even whether someone has ever chosen to study such a thing, I do not know. But it was the kind of wisdom that came from a lifetime of observation, and nature tends to make all of us open our eyes and think.

My father also believed that you ate what you killed, and so my mother had a number of recipes that fit both rabbit and squirrel interchangeably. Sometimes we just ate the meat broiled with a side of sliced tomatoes or homemade pickles. Other times it was stewed. More often, it was fried.

It might not sound like much, but it was pretty good. My father would also usually get a couple of deer during the hunting season, which was the legal limit. We would eat every bit that was edible, and that could take quite a while. Dad was terrific with a shotgun, so we spent many a time cleaning, then eating, ducks and quail.

In the nature around my house I learned life lessons—an overworked phrase, I grant you, but an apt one. When I was nine years old, my friends and I came across a giant soft-shell turtle in the Buffalo Bayou. It was the biggest one we had ever seen, and we spent the entire day tracking it. After many foiled attempts, we finally snared it, bound it up, and walked back the mile or so to my parents' house. We filled a tub with water in the backyard and put it in. We felt like conquering heroes, but that only lasted until my father came home from work. When he saw what we had done, he was furious and explained to me how such behavior could harm a wild animal like this turtle. Even though it was after dark, he insisted that I carry the turtle back to where we'd found it. Now, this wasn't the equivalent of a valiant effort to save an endangered species, but my father's instinct was the same: Nature was not there for us to exploit or toy with. It is a lesson I have never forgotten.

Going into the forest with my dad was a backdrop to my young life. It was just what people did. I was expected to be able to identify the species of trees and to know how to avoid getting lost. Nature wasn't something that you drove to, or planned on seeing, or for which you bought a fancy outdoor wardrobe. I worry that now it is an activity that must compete with soccer practices, homework, piano lessons, and all the other responsibilities that fill up the calendar of a family with children. All those are surely wonderful and rewarding, but so too is just letting your legs wander through the trees and meadows, and having your mind wander as well.

Today most of us encounter few animals and plants in our daily lives, and most of what we do see are either the ones we have domesticated or the vermin and weeds that can thrive in the cracks of modernity. Growing up I was enthralled by the night sky. But now most of us can see only a few faint stars at night, the ones bright enough to make it through the domes of light that enclose our metropolises. For all of human history, the night sky told stories, delineated time, and guided voyagers. Now 30 percent of the people on the planet can't even see the Milky Way from their homes. And in the United States, 80 percent of us can't.

We as a nation have done much to exploit the land, despoil it, and pollute it. From wildlife to wildfires, we have been shortsighted in our management. For too long the cost of doing business ignored the cost of that business to the environment. Still, we have been world leaders in conservation, preservation, and environmentalism. And that is what makes this moment in time so baffling and worrisome. Somehow the environment has become yet another point of contention between Democrats and Republicans. It is striking that those who live in urban centers and are more isolated from the natural world tend to vote for Democratic candidates who mostly favor stricter environmental regulations. Meanwhile, those in rural areas tend to vote for Republican candidates who more often advocate for laxer oversight of land, water, and pollution. I am not exactly sure how this came to be. Some of it likely has to do with the coarsening of dialogue between the two major parties on almost every issue, and ultimately the environment gets sorted along those binary lines as well. Research also suggests that those states whose economies are built on oil, gas, coal, and mining tend to be less likely to support environmental regulations, and understandably so. But whatever the cause, it is important to note that these political and social divides over the environment were not always this way.

It was an odd experience watching the heated debate as a cap and trade bill for carbon dioxide emissions and climate change made its way through Congress in 2009. The opposition from Republicans was fierce, with only a handful voting for final passage in the House of Representatives.

Dozens of Democrats in conservative districts also voted against the bill. In the end, the legislation barely passed the House and was never even brought up in the Senate. And yet the very idea of cap and trade as a way to deal with environmental problems, where you set limits and allow polluters to trade in credits, had been the brainchild of Republicans. President Ronald Reagan had used cap and trade to phase out lead in gasoline, and President George H. W. Bush had used it to cut the pollutants causing acid rain.

When I sat down recently with George Shultz, who had served as secretary of state under President Reagan, he spoke with pride of the Republican legacy on the environment, stretching back to President Theodore Roosevelt. Secretary Shultz has become a vocal advocate for protecting the planet against climate change, and he reminded me that major environmental progress—from the founding of the EPA to tackling the ozone and acid rain problems, to strengthening clean water and air acts—had happened under Republican administrations.

Questions of the environment boil down to acts of leadership. Most people would say that they want clean air and water. The concerns that you hear about pitting economic growth against environmental protections are legitimate; we need a balanced approach. Our modern lives require that we mine, till, fish, generate electricity, and discard refuse.

We will never return to some mythic state of environmental purity. Nor would we want to. But that doesn't mean we can't be wiser about how we use our limited resources and protect our planet. I believe that if there was leadership on this issue in both political parties, the American people would rally to action.

We humans seem to have a hard time measuring risk. We can see the dangers in the moment, but threats that stretch over the course of generations are hard for us to judge, let alone act to remedy. Climate change is just such a problem. Even though we already see very worrisome fluctuations in Earth's functions—extreme weather, vanishing sea ice, rising temperatures, and rising oceans—the most dire effects will not strike with full force until well after I am gone. We can hide from the truth for now, but it will not last. In my interview with Secretary Shultz, he described climate change as a clear and present danger even if many of his fellow Republicans do not see it that way. I asked him how he felt about this state of affairs. He said those who deny climate change now will ultimately be "mugged by reality." *Mugged by reality.* It is a strong phrase. The danger is that when the climate deniers are finally mugged, it will be, by definition, too late. Already we are seeing the glaciers melt in Greenland and massive ice sheets breaking off Antarctica.

Often I find myself thinking back to my boyhood out in the forests and meadows and how those experiences spurred in me a love of our natural world. One of the joys of my later life has been the summer days I spend in quiet contentment fishing in the upper Beaverkill River in the Catskill mountain range of western New York State. My eyes are mostly focused on the action in the stream, watching the currents and eddies, casting flies, looking for trout willing to bite. But I often glance up to contemplate the flora and fauna of the riverbank—particularly the birch trees that are rooted just on the edge of the water. They favor the embankments in many northern climes, and sometimes, as I take in the scene, an old African American spiritual comes to mind. I begin singing slowly, "Just like a tree planted by the water, I shall not be moved. I shall not be, I shall not be moved. . . ." The hymn may say I shall not be moved, but I often am, in that strange and mystical way engaging in nature often moves us.

There is an elegance to birches, tall and slender, with their distinctive white bark. I've always liked them because my long-departed mother loved them so. Born, raised, and buried on the semitropical Texas Gulf Coast, she never saw a live birch, only pictures in a book. Mother's favorite tree, however, was the native magnolia, which flourishes all along the Texas Gulf Coast and adjacent piney woods. She loved their strength and the fragrance of their large white blossoms. That scent permeating and enveloping in the heavy humidity of Texas nights is among the fondest memories of my childhood. I smell it often, even when a magnolia is nowhere in sight.

I like to sit out there on the river for a long while, and take a deep breath and close my eyes. Nature doesn't please only our sense of sight. I can hear the soothing sounds of running water and swaying leaves in the background. Nature has the power to inspire one's mind and move one's soul like great music or poetry. It can fill you with humility when you encounter the otherworldliness of the Grand Canyon. It can fill you with awe when you tilt your head back and try to tease out the top of a towering redwood. It can spark your imagination as you try to visualize a time when the entire continent was as wild as Michigan's Upper Peninsula. And it can fill you with sadness when you see how much the glaciers in Glacier National Park are receding. What are we doing? What have we done?

I am an optimist by nature, and I believe we can find a will to save the planet. We have a strong and growing environmental sensibility in this country and around the world—especially among the young. But there are hurdles, not the least of which come from many of our elected officials. We have seen the undue influence of big money from the fossil fuel industry, along with their allies in government, actively undermine climate science. We have seen crises like what has taken place in Flint, Michigan, call into question our national commitment to equal access to clean water and air. To the countless generations yet to be born, what world will we leave for them? We have seen that we can make progress and repair damage to the environment. But now, when it is needed with an urgency we haven't really seen before, we are blinking. How can we open our eyes once again to the notion of a fragile planet, our only home?

*Apollo 8* was on its fourth pass around the moon when the commander, Frank Borman, initiated a scheduled roll of the spacecraft. On the audio recordings, you can hear William Anders, who was the lunar module's pilot, react to a sight no human had ever seen before: "Oh my God! Look at that picture over there! There's the earth coming up. Wow, is that pretty." Anders called out to the third crew member, Jim Lovell, asking if he had color film. There was a scramble inside the spacecraft to get the picture taken before it was too late. They got their shot.

The astronauts were not looking for Earth when they went on their mission. The space historian Andrew Chaikin said Anders told him later, "We were trained to go to the moon. We were focused on the moon, observing the moon, studying the moon, and the earth was not really in our thoughts until it popped up above that horizon." We need this vision of a unified and cohesive Earth to pop up once again over the horizon of our global complacency. We need to consider, with awe and humility, the future of our fragile home.

# Public Education

When I entered first grade in 1937, Texas was still mostly rural, and Houston was a far cry from the sprawling metropolis it is to-day. William G. Love Elementary School was in one of the poorer sections of town, but it was rich in leadership and dedicated, talented teachers. All of them were women. In that period, with few exceptions, the only work outside the home open to a woman was as a nurse, a secretary, a waitress, or a teacher. And teaching was an option for only the comparatively few women who had finished college. So it is no wonder that Love Elementary, in the heart of "the wrong part of town," was loaded not just with women, but with very smart, hardworking women.

The principal, Mrs. Simmons, was the smartest, hardest-working of them all, and she was a potent force in my early life. With the exception of my parents, she probably did more than anyone else to shape me into the person I would become. Mrs. Simmons ran her school as a kind of benevolent dictatorship. She personally hired every teacher. She knew every student's name. She was in and out of all the classrooms every day, checking, directing, encouraging, and spreading her creed of "Love conquers all." It was a play on the school's name, of course, but it also formed the basis for her mantra: "We all love to learn and we love one another."

Don't be misled by all this talk of "love," however. School under Mrs. Simmons was a protective place, but you weren't coddled. She was a tough disciplinarian who had zero tolerance for any misbehavior. If you acted up in class, got into a shoving match on the playground, or disrespected a teacher, you wound up in Mrs. Simmons's office. She would sit in her over-large upholstered chair behind her spartan desk, and you would sit on the single wooden chair before it. The Texas and American flags stood imposingly in each corner, and the mottled light filtered in through the two large oak trees behind her windows. It was the last place any kid wanted to be.

Mrs. Simmons would tell you in no uncertain terms of your punishment, and then she would call or write your parents. In our neighborhood, few people could afford telephones, and if they had a phone, they had only "party line" service, sharing their line with many other households. These phones were often busy, so Mrs. Simmons usually sent notes home. The notes would encourage (actually, require) your parents to come in for a chat. She minced no words. When she felt it was needed, she would remind you and your parents that her natural decency and kindness (her "Love conquers all") should not be misunderstood; she could be—and, when necessary, would be—a lioness. Sometimes, to both break the ice and make a point, she would explain, "You know, there's tough. There's street tough—Heights tough . . . and then there is prison tough." After a pause, she would invariably add, in a voice I can still remember, "And trust me, friends, I can be prison tough and beyond if I have to be." She was joking, overstating, but not by much. Her talks were especially popular with fathers in the neighborhood. She spoke their language.

Mrs. Simmons and all the teachers lived in better neighborhoods than the Heights. Every day they would come to Love Elementary almost as if they were descending the social strata of Houston. You could tell this by how they dressed, in nicer clothes than what most of our families could afford. But more so, you could tell it in the way they spoke, with less of an accent. They didn't drop their g's (they were "going" somewhere, not "goin'"), and they didn't turn their *e*'s into *i*'s (if you asked my friends how old they were in fifth grade, they would have said "tin"). But you never felt condescended to. All the teachers had a deep love for not only their students and parents, but also for our community, city, state, and country. I like to think these patriotic instincts are some of the same that prompt our best teachers to answer their calling.

I grew up at a time when regional identity was far greater than it is today, particularly in proud, independent Texas, but we were clearly being trained to be full and active citizens in these broader United States. We learned and reveled in the uniqueness of being American even as the world outside our school doors was mired in the Great Depression and World War II. However, we were also blind to the profound injustice of learning about the greatness of the United States as students in an all-white school. I didn't even know where the nearest African American elementary school was for most of my childhood. The first time I ever saw it was in high school, when some African American kids I played street baseball with invited me to an outdoor party in their neighborhood. Walking there, I passed the elementary school. It was small and run-down, and didn't have much of a school yard.

Despite this glaring deficit on race, my elementary school

education started to give me the tools to understand my country, a path that would eventually allow me to realize America's injustices as well as its strengths. Our teachers were true believers in the American Dream, and they drilled it into our impressionable minds all through elementary school: "Dream . . . you can do it," they'd say, "but only if you study and work hard." We discussed the meaning of the phrase "one nation, indivisible" as early as second grade and frequently in the years that followed. (It should be noted that the phrase "under God" was not added to the Pledge of Allegiance until the Cold War, after I had graduated from college.)

I was the first in my family ever to enter an institution of higher learning, and with our household income I was destined to attend a public college. Sam Houston State Teachers College in Huntsville, Texas, had a small, rural campus hidden behind pine trees. There was no ivy anywhere in sight. We didn't have alumni who were presidents or Supreme Court justices. We weren't a major athletic power or an academic powerhouse. My classmates and I didn't have very lofty ambitions, but they seemed atmospheric at the time. We were college students and the pride in that was palpable. Many of my classmates were, like me, from Texas families who had never sent anyone to college. A large number of the male students had their tuition covered by the GI Bill.

As a country we were determined to knock down the doors to the middle class, rebuild our nation, and use education as a ladder for not only our own growth but also for future generations.

My college was full of dedicated educators who might not have had national reputations for the quality of their scholarship, but who were committed to teaching us with an idealism that today may sound a bit corny or unbelievable. As professors at a teachers college, their job was to train the educators of the future, to pass on the torch of their own chosen career. Maybe it was because we were in the immediate wake of World War II, maybe it was because of the older students who had seen service in that war, but for whatever reason there was a real spirit among even those of us who were young and immature that attending college was not just a rite of passage. Education was a gift, part of the panoply of blessings for having the good luck to be alive at that time and in those United States. The classes that really stood out for me were those in the new sociology department. Under the guise of explaining how modern cities worked, those professors also carefully broached the issue of race, and the disparities of segregated schools.

In hindsight, and with the clarity provided by the intervening years, I can see some of the limitations of my teachers, in their experiences and worldviews. We didn't learn much about foreign cultures, let alone appreciate the different cultures within our own nation. Our literary canon was composed almost exclusively of white, mostly male authors. There was very little discussion about the great sins of our own history, even slavery, let alone the plight of Native Americans, religious minorities, and other marginalized groups. We didn't appreciate the full importance of science or the need to protect the environment. Outside the classroom, we were far less sophisticated in identifying bullying and other forms of abuse. Even in the amber glow of nostalgia, my schools were a long way from perfect.

When I became a reporter, it didn't take long for me to see how many of the inequities in our nation were grounded in the limitations of our educational system. I was on assignment as a fresh-faced correspondent for CBS News in the fall of 1962 when James Meredith bravely attempted to integrate the University of Mississippi, and while I knew the situation would be tense, I was not prepared for what followed. No one was. Just a few years removed from my own cherished college experience, I was deeply disturbed to be on a college campus, a beautiful one with a deep history, and see the hate for a man whose crime was that he simply wanted an education. It is too easy for those who today breezily dismiss the legacy of race and education to forget what happened in places like Oxford. Thousands of students and outside agitators were whipped into a murderous fury. Federal troops brought in to keep the peace confronted a riot of gunfire and arson, and two civilians were murdered. We still are living in the shadow of this history. Over the years that followed, I would report on many stories that portrayed the great and dire inconsistencies in our public education systems. I would see it on Native American reservations and in dying rural communities and poor neighborhoods. I would see it in the ostracism of marginalized groups within schools and the struggles that young women faced to overcome academic exclusion and alienation.

Despite all these injustices, I still had the sense for most of my early career that by and large public education was on a steady march of progress, fueled by a spirit of bipartisan support. Recently I have begun to despair, as I see the very notion of public schools under threat. Instead of a national will to make free and open education a priority and strength, I see insidious forces overtly and covertly undermining our public schools.

The crisis of our schools, especially public schools, is complex. And difficult questions abound: Does the general school tax system need to be reevaluated or not? How do we assess the impact of charter schools, and are some voucher systems worthy of consideration? What about Wall Street's increasing involvement in for-profit schools? What is the optimum role for teachers' unions? The list goes on. But there should be no dispute that if American schools don't improve, America will lose its world leadership. And I believe that whatever system emerges in the future, it must hew to our ideals of public education: It must be open to all, free of charge, and of the highest quality.

Instead, what we are seeing is a persistent (and in some cases increasing) de facto segregation of schools along fissures of race and economic class, between urban and suburban districts, as well as within cities themselves. We see rising tuitions at public universities and the under-resourcing of community colleges, one of the unheralded backbones of our educational community. We see educational standards based more on politics than on pedagogy. And when it comes to training future generations, there are few professions more important than teaching, and yet teachers are compensated at levels out of balance with their responsibilities.

During my travels to other countries, I have seen that they approach their public school systems differently. While our schools are mired in inconsistency and often plagued by poor performance, many of the world's industrialized countries are achieving superior results. This is one of the most important news stories of our time, and I have been interested in understanding how other nations do it, so a few years back, my reporting team and I decided to compare two very different countries whose schools are highly acclaimed.

In Finland, children spend less time in class than almost any other developed country. They are given tremendous amounts of freedom and have very little homework. Public schools cater to everyone; there are almost no private schools in the entire country. In Finland, it isn't just the best students who do well. The country's commitment to building a system where every child, regardless of circumstance, has access to a good school has produced impressive results. Finland's students regularly score among the highest in the world.

In Singapore, where students are also among the world's highest scorers, schools are strict and rigid. Whereas there are very few standardized tests in Finland, in Singapore they form the basis for the educational system. The tests (multiple-choice exams, in addition to written and oral exams) help sort students into elite academic colleges, technical schools, or vocational training. These tests are so important that more than 90 percent of Singaporean students get private tutoring after school or on weekends to prepare.

Although Singapore and Finland are polar opposites in

their educational philosophies, they have some important similarities besides just the high results for their students. Both countries have come a long way, fast. As late as the 1950s, Finland's economy was largely agrarian and stagnant, until the country's leaders made a commitment to educate every child. In Singapore in 1965, an estimated 40 percent of the population was illiterate, but then the country's leaders undertook a radical educational overhaul. So both Finland and Singapore have a rigorous commitment from their national governments to make quality schools, evenly distributed in their population, a top priority. And there is another important key to their success: Schoolteachers are held in high esteem in both countries, and they get a lot of training and support.

Given the current struggles within the United States, it may be hard to remember that up until relatively recently our school system was the envy of the world. That was an outgrowth of our changing country, for while some public schools existed early on, it was really the rise of educational reformers in the antebellum era that set us on the path to true public education. Few loom larger than Horace Mann, who argued that a truly free populace could not remain ignorant, and that communities must provide nonsectarian public schools, staffed by trained teachers and open to students of diverse backgrounds. His reforms for primary and eventually secondary education, begun in Massachusetts, soon spread to other parts of the country, especially as the nation was shifting from an agricultural to an industrial economy, and from rural areas to cities.

The United States has also historically been a leader in public education at the college and university level. Before the Civil War, higher education was an opportunity that was available to only a tiny fraction of the population. But as the nation grew, America needed a better-trained citizenry to compete in the industrial age. So in 1862, in the midst of the Civil War, Congress passed and President Lincoln signed the Morrill Act, which set up the land grant college system. States were given federal land to either use or sell to establish the "endowment, support, and maintenance of at least one college where the leading object shall be, without excluding other scientific and classical studies, and including military tactics, to teach such branches of learning as are related to agriculture and the mechanic arts." These schools would be focused on agriculture and engineering, but they would really become general universities—schools such as the University of California, the University of Nebraska, the Ohio State University, and many others. The states viewed higher education as a central governmental service they would provide to their citizens. I, and millions of others like me, benefited from this civic mission.

Despite this broad national effort to expand access to education, local and state control of schools and state colleges has always been a pillar of our system. In a positive sense, this has allowed our schools to more nimbly respond to the needs of our communities—such as in California, one of the most diverse states in the Union, which recently passed a law that will create ethnic studies classes in high schools. It's not just curriculum; having differing state policies on education provides diverse laboratories for innovation.

But all the advantages of this decentralized system are predicated on state and local governments believing in the importance of funding high-quality education, an instinct that is in steep decline in many places. A system of local control can also distribute funding unfairly, as we see often today when rich suburban districts have resources that poorer and urban ones do not.

Since local control also gives communities great power to shape curriculum, whether it is teaching about evolution, civil rights history, or climate change, the hyper-partisanship of our nation is trickling into the classroom. In several states, boards of education have adopted standards that undermine the futures of the very students these schools are supposed to serve. My beloved state of Texas has been a particularly egregious example, where new guidelines for textbooks have even downplayed the role of slavery as the cause of the Civil War. The reactionary wing of the American political spectrum is making its mark in this arena, and to great effect. And because schools are controlled on a local level, the federal government is hard pressed, and often resistant, to step in to address curriculum issues. But the fight for the soul of American public education is one from which none of us can afford to shrink. It is in essence a battle for the heart, soul, and future of the United States.

One of the great strengths of the public education system is that it provides a world of second chances. I have seen many late bloomers struggle in their early years at school and later go on to a community college and transfer to a four-year school. Education is not about just planting a seed; it is also about nurturing, over many decades, a productive, meaningful, and happy life.

One of my most vivid memories from Love Elementary School was how the now-overlooked Arbor Day holiday was always a marked occasion on the school calendar. Mrs. Simmons would take a great personal interest, directing the yearly activity of planting a tree on the school grounds. Each year we would gather around to see a delicate sapling go into the soil. Our responsibilities had but just begun. We were formed into rotating teams in the months after the planting, tasked with nourishing the young trees into maturity. We took that job very seriously, an instinct I would like to think we learned from our teachers.

On a recent trip to Houston with one of my grandsons, we drove past my old school. In many ways it looked the same as when I had gone there, and as we paused for a moment I could see the echoes of my much younger self. Each school day, Love Elementary is once again filled with girls and boys who have their entire lives ahead of them. They will grow, and they will have to be nurtured. I was happy to see that five of the six trees we students planted during my time at the school remained standing. There was that marvelous magnolia. There was one of the solid oaks. I thought of what a wonderful metaphor these trees were for education. They were planted as an investment in the future. They have weathered many storms to provide shade to the generations who followed me. They stood tall, and proud. They had taken root and been allowed to thrive under a canopy of love. And so had I.

# Service

**M**any memories will die when those of us who remember the Second World War pass on: the shock of Pearl Harbor, the shifting fortunes in the European and Pacific theaters, the dawning horror of the full scope of the Holocaust. But less dramatic and more personal memories will also disappear forever, like our emotional response to the American war songs that were produced to comfort and rally a nation. To later generations, those songs of the early 1940s, with their simple tunes and lyrics that verge on (or sometimes even surpass) the jingoistic, may at best rise to the level of intellectual curiosity. But if I hear just a few bars of many of them, my eyes sometimes dampen, and it's hard to sing the lyrics without a quiver in my voice.

The words and music transport me back. I remember so many neighbors waiting nervously for news of loved ones fighting in battles overseas; I remember mourning parents, children left without fathers; and I remember the knocks on doors that changed lives in an instant. The world of my youth was engulfed in a desperate fight for the survival of humanity, but these songs remind me that we remained in some ways oddly innocent. Simple songs of heroism and sacrifice, with evocative titles like "There's a Star Spangled Banner Waving Somewhere," were welcomed and embraced by a grateful public without cynicism.

There is one song that still strikes at me harder than most, "The Ballad of Rodger Young." It tells the story of a young infantryman who gave his life so that his fellow soldiers could live. Young was a man short in stature but big in heart. Despite his size, he had been a star athlete in high school, until a basketball head injury left him almost deaf. After dropping out of school, he enlisted in the Ohio National Guard and was sent to the Pacific. He rose to the rank of sergeant, but asked to be demoted to private because he could not hear well enough to lead his men into battle. In an ambush in the Solomon Islands on July 31, 1943, Young charged a Japanese pillbox. The citation for his posthumous Congressional Medal of Honor tells of how he was shot twice by machine-gun fire during his push up the hill, and yet "he continued his heroic advance, attracting enemy fire and answering with rifle fire. . . . He began throwing hand grenades, and while doing so was hit again and killed." Young had recently turned twenty-five years old. His is a story of uncommon valor, but in war, I have found, such stories are not uncommon.

What shakes me to the core in this song is the fourth stanza, which paints a picture of Young's final resting place:

> On the island of New Georgia in the Solomons
> Stands a simple wooden cross alone to tell
> That beneath the silent coral of the Solomons
> Sleeps a man, sleeps a man remembered well.

These words capture the heroism and insanity of war writ large. Who had ever heard of the Solomon Islands? And yet young men were sent to die there for a cause much larger than themselves, just as they were sent to die in the deserts of North Africa, the high seas of the Pacific, the mountain villages of Italy, and so many other distant battlefields. This is not just the story of World War II, of course, but of all wars, across all time.

We live in debt to those who have served and died, a debt tallied in blood. And too often our political leaders who commit our young men, and now young women, into war do not take this truth into account with an adequate fullness of measure. Over the years, I have been to many military cemeteries, and I am always overcome with waves of emotion. This is especially true of the cemeteries that are filled, not with the tombs of long-lived veterans who earned a military burial for their service, but with the graves of the young who perished in battle. For me the most striking hallowed ground is the Normandy American Cemetery in France. I defy anyone to walk through its more than 170 acres of green grass and white crosses and stars and not feel deeply moved. All told, 9,387 American servicemen are buried there, with uniform grave markers, regardless of the rank they held in life. Death strikes us all with the same finality.

The cemetery is one of the most peaceful and beautiful places I have ever visited—a far cry from the pain and torment that led to its creation. Most buried there lost their lives in that fateful landing on the nearby beaches on D-day or in the fierce battles that immediately followed. I am struck by their ages. You quickly do the math, subtracting date of birth from date of death, and invariably arrive at a number in the high teens or early twenties. You cannot help but think: What might they have accomplished if they had lived? What happened to the loved ones they left behind?

Another striking cemetery can be found halfway around

the globe, in a volcanic crater in the hills above Honolulu. Nicknamed Punchbowl, it is a tribute to the sacrifice in our Pacific and Asian wars, not only World War II, but also Korea and Vietnam. Above the bustle of Waikiki, it is a place for meditation on the cost of service with the "courts of the missing"—walls of 28,808 names etched in marble of those who went missing in action or were lost and buried at sea. As an inscription at the cemetery reminds us: "In these gardens are recorded the names of Americans who gave their lives in the service of their country and whose earthly resting place is known only to God." "Known only to God" is a phrase that epitomizes a level of service beyond our full comprehension. In war, most deaths are lonely, and leave loneliness behind.

War turns upside down the normal order of life; being young makes you more likely to die. The attack on Pearl Harbor took place on a Sunday, and I remember my father and his younger brother John going immediately to the recruiting office in downtown Houston. When they arrived, the lines were already long and the office hadn't yet opened. Most were eventually told to just wait and that the military would be in touch. My father, already in his thirties with three young children and doing what was deemed essential work in the oil fields, would not end up on active military duty (he later volunteered for the civil defense units and became our neighborhood civil watch). My uncle John, already in his late twenties and with flat, slightly deformed feet, also didn't go off to war. Their offers to volunteer for active military service were declined. My uncle Hartzell Sherrill, who was young and single, volunteered for the navy. He was the quintessential taciturn Texan, and he ended up in the merchant marines. It was the kind of service that did not get the attention or glory it deserved, although as I have since learned in my years reporting on wars, some of the bravest members of our military are the ones who serve in a role supporting those on the front lines. My uncle carried out "suicide runs" to Murmansk, arctic convoys that sent desperately needed supplies to our then allies in the Soviet Union. These were dangerous assignments and dozens of ships were sunk. Uncle Hartzell survived, but he didn't get many medals for his courageous service, and when he returned he didn't talk about it much. That was common as well.

And that is how it was during World War II: There was a sense of service that permeated all of society, even down to young boys like me. I remember the rationing of food and materials. The idea that we all had to go without, that we were all asked to sacrifice in even small ways, created a sense of togetherness. It was everyone's war, and everyone was encouraged to participate. The government sponsored drives to collect spare aluminum, rubber, and the like. Looking back now, I am not sure if all this was actually needed for the war effort, or whether these drives, organized down to the neighborhood level, were meant simply to inspire a unity of purpose. Whatever the reason, my young friends and I were hooked. We would scour the creeks and bayous near our homes for discarded junk. And when I collected more than any other kid in the neighborhood, I was awarded a little ribbon with what I now know to be a cheap metal disk. But to my much younger self it was an important medal, bestowed, I was told, by none other than General Dwight D. Eisenhower himself. Of course there were kids all over town, and across the country, who received the same thing. But to be decorated by the commander of Allied forces in Europe was a big source of pride. And that medal became a prized possession.

What that early experience taught me is that service can come in many forms. Now we, as a nation, are in desperate need of expanding and celebrating the notion of service. As a journalist I often confront the Dickensian side of life—in places like prisons, county hospitals, police stations, and homeless shelters. I see despair, desperation, and piercing cruelty—enough to often lead me to question the decency of my fellow man. But I am also struck by the many men and women I find of deep service: doctors, nurses, clerks, social workers, paramedics, police officers, district attorneys, public defenders, and so on. Not everyone I have met in these positions is perfect; far from it. But the vast majority are committed to their work and to making difficult and painful situations less difficult and painful.

And then there are those I've met in my travels around the United States who give of themselves every day to strengthen their communities. They are teachers, firefighters, and guidance counselors. They volunteer in nursing homes and youth centers. They are part of an America of largely unapplauded service, but most who do this work have no interest in seeking recognition. They understand that each act of assistance is a vote of confidence in our common humanity.

I am proud that both of my children went into careers of public service, giving up more lucrative paths to help their communities—my son, first as a public defender and now as an assistant district attorney, and my daughter as a leader in environmental and civic causes. My wife, Jean, has provided an example, volunteering for years and bringing children with learning disabilities and from underprivileged homes into our own home to teach them how to read. None of my family members will tell you that they should be recognized for their actions. They understand that they are blessed with much and that others do far more. They see all this as their duty to country. This is how widespread and common service really is.

The act of service is rooted in the purest of our democratic impulses. After we married, I often traveled with Jean to visit her family in Smithville, Texas, and one favorite activity was sitting in on the town's council meetings, on which my father-in-law served. The council was made up of farmers, small-business owners, and teachers who were elected in nonpartisan elections. I would watch these earnest men and women follow Robert's Rules of Order and debate substantial local concerns, whether it was to buy a new police car or lay a new water pipe. This was bottom-up democracy, infused with real public service. And it was a beautiful sight to behold.

Perhaps it is not controversial to write glowingly of small-town democracy resembling a scene from a Norman Rockwell painting, but truthfully, this same sense of purpose and service fills our great capital city. "Washington" has become for many a dirty word that connotes self-serving politicians and devious lobbyists. To be sure, they are there, but I remember when I first went to work in the city in the wake of the Kennedy assassination, being struck by how populated the government was with young people from every corner of the nation, there to do the right thing and serve their country. I still feel that way whenever I return. Yes, you see ambition, but also idealism and the desire to work hard. You see purpose and patriotism. It is bipartisan. This is a part of Washington that doesn't get nearly enough attention.

It isn't just the young and idealistic. Walk past the Department of Justice, Agriculture, Treasury, or any of the other government agencies at the end of the workday. Watch the men and women stream out in large numbers. Many of them could earn a better salary for less work in the private sector, yet they work here because they believe in service to country. When politicians call our government workers lazy or ineffectual, it is often for cynical political gain. Can government bureaucracies be infuriating and inefficient? Of course. But so can any big organization, whether it be a labor union, a nonprofit, or a private enterprise. Have you ever waited on the phone for an airline or cable company? To be sure, there are problems with Washington, but most of them can be found on Capitol Hill and K Street and in the White House, not in the windowless offices of the Environmental Protection Agency or the State Department.

And then there are all the Americans serving around the globe, representing our nation in official and unofficial capacities. There is our diplomatic corps, not only the political ambassadors, but often more impressively the career workers—the quiet Americans—who toil in difficult and sometimes dangerous locales with little to no recognition for their service. There are the Peace Corps volunteers and leaders of nongovernmental organizations who build schools, treat disease, and deliver clean water. Service to our country is about not only helping us and ours, but also taking care of others around the world. In 2004, just after most of us had gone to bed on Christmas, a massive earthquake shook the Indian Ocean and triggered a tsunami that reached such heights and wreaked such horrors it is almost impossible to comprehend. We will never know the exact loss of life, but it is estimated in excess of 230,000 people. Entire towns were wiped off the map. The rest of the world, preoccupied with end-of-year celebrations, was slow to react. Even at CBS News, I had to convince the president of the news division that this was worthy of intensive coverage.

On December 31, I was on a plane for *60 Minutes*, along with my producers Chris Martin and Elliot Kirschner. The United States military had dispatched the aircraft carrier USS *Abraham Lincoln* to the waters off the coast of the Indonesian island of Sumatra. We landed on January 2 on the carrier deck, which was already a beehive of activity as its helicopters were airlifting supplies around the clock. The next morning we took off for the disaster zone. Out my window I could see beautifully vegetated coastlines of steep cliffs, but the trees and plants didn't reach the sea. Instead, there was a tall band of brown dirt. The wall of water, perhaps as high as eighty to a hundred feet, had struck with such force that it ripped away everything in its path.

We touched down on a big grassy field, and I met Americans of all types, from the foreign service, the United States Agency for International Development (USAID), and many others. They were confronting death at a scale I had never seen in a land bereft of services. We took off with supplies for the nearby regional capital of Banda Aceh, where tens of thousands of people had lost their lives. Those who had managed to survive had been cut off for days, undoubtedly wondering if help would ever come. The first outsiders they saw were young Americans handing out food and medicine provided by the U.S. government. It was one of the most difficult stories I have ever covered, but my spirits were soothed slightly by witnessing this level of dedicated service from my countrymen and -women.

It would benefit our republic greatly if we saw these instincts for service more often in our elected officials. There was a time when some form of military service was almost a prerequisite for politicians. While I have great respect for the military, I do not think that should be the only service recognized. But our society would benefit if more of our politicians had at least shown some inclination toward personal sacrifice and the need to help others before they entered office. At a time when we see many elected officials skirting their own scant history of service, military or otherwise, it is nice to meet young men like Seth Moulton.

Moulton is a product of a fancy boarding school who has a degree in physics from Harvard. But he completed four tours in Iraq as a marine officer in combat when he could have had a far easier and more comfortable life. I first met Moulton while reporting on the Iraq War, and as I got to know him over the years, it was clear he felt a deep need to serve. When he decided to mount a primary challenge to a long-sitting Democratic congressman in his Massachusetts district in 2014, I wasn't sure if he could knock off the establishment. He did, and he went on to win the general election. During the campaign, it was revealed in the *Boston Globe* that Moulton had received numerous combat medals in Iraq for his service, including the Bronze Star. And he hadn't even told his parents. "There is a healthy disrespect among veterans who served on the front lines for people who walk around telling war stories," Moulton told the *Globe*. There were "many others who did heroic things and received no awards at all."

How many politicians could you imagine approaching their accomplishments with this level of humility, especially among our current leaders? That is the benefit of service: It tends to humanize you. People can disagree politically and philosophically on all the issues that confront our nation, but if more of our elected officials had served in causes other than their own advancement, I believe they would approach their jobs with less certainty in their own assumptions and more sympathy for the needs of others. It matters less whether it's in the military, the Peace Corps, the many programs of AmeriCorps, social services, or legal aid. It's about the values that drive a person to help by joining a mission that is bigger than they are.

When politicians from their gilded perch in Washington cut funding for foreign aid programs, I am troubled. When they denigrate government workers, I am indignant. And when they send the men and women who volunteered for our armed forces to multiple tours of combat while asking nothing of sacrifice from the rest of us, I am angry. We either choose to be part of a community that stretches beyond ourselves, our material needs, and our creature comforts, or we do not. In our society, it is possible for the selfish and self-centered to live at the expense of the rest of the population. We live in an age where such attitudes are conspicuously apparent. Thankfully most people I have met have chosen to give back to their communities, in ways big and small. On a personal level, service may be considered a virtue. But in a democratic society such as ours, we must consider it a necessity.

# CHARACTER

★ ★ ★

# Audacity

I t was Abraham Lincoln who authorized the first transcontinental railroad during the Civil War. How audacious. By the time I was born, architecturally stunning train stations bustled at the heart of almost every American city, and as a child I would marvel at the mighty locomotives pulling the nation forward in their billowing wake. I'm old enough to remember with fondness the original Penn Station in New York City, which was modeled on one of the great ruins of Rome. While those ruins remain today, the old Penn Station does not—having been demolished in the 1960s, ostensibly in the service of progress.

I still love taking the train, but I now have to leave New York through the new Penn Station, one of the most dispiriting public buildings in America. It's a warren of dirty underground hallways, and it embodies the opposite of audacity; it is utilitarian, cost-beneficial, and utterly uninspired. Comparing the old Penn Station to the new, Yale architecture professor Vincent Scully Jr. lamented, "One entered the city like a god; one scuttles in now like a rat." And while I like to ride Amtrak's high-speed Acela line, it is also a bit disappointing—a reminder that the United States long ago lost its lead on rail to the great trains of Europe and Asia.

My work often takes me to Washington, D.C., and as I pull into the beautifully renovated Union Station, I begin to feel better. I emerge to see the mighty Capitol dome, and I wonder: *If we were building the Capitol today, would we make it so bold and beautiful?* Its stateliness embodied the audacity of a nation. In its chambers were passed laws of sweeping import. More recently, it has been largely a house of small-mindedness, as politicians have maintained power by essentially promising to take government out of the business of big ideas.

American greatness has largely been driven by audacity. Thirteen far-flung colonies challenged, and defeated, the mighty British army. A Constitution written more than two centuries ago has outlined a stable form of government. A multiracial and multiethnic nation is a source of strength. A free and open society has allowed us to push the boundaries of human knowledge and exploration.

I often think about this national proclivity toward bold-ness when I step out on the porch of my favorite fishing cabin and look to the sparkling night sky. Seeing all those stars and a brilliant moon, I reflect on how, during my child-hood, the idea of travel into the heavens existed only in the imagination of fiction writers such as Jules Verne. But then we sent a man to the moon, launched robotic explorations to Mars, and, with the *Voyager* spacecrafts, have now sent beacons of our species beyond the bounds of our own solar system. How audacious.

Today the space dreamers that capture public attention are private-sector mavericks such as Elon Musk and Richard Branson, whose goals keep us relatively close to Earth. Al-though NASA still boasts brilliant scientists and determined public servants, it increasingly has faded from public view into just another quiet governmental bureaucracy. Some-how the desire for bold exploration has ebbed among our elected officials.

I remember a time when roads were bumpy and often unpaved. Then we built a network of highways that opened up the United States to the ease and convenience of travel that had been unimaginable, until it became a reality. The investment in our infrastructure has had incalculable bene-fits to commerce and mobility. How audacious we were. But now I see crumbling roads and bridges wherever I go. Time has taken its toll on the concrete and asphalt beds, but it has taken an even bigger toll on our national ambition.

It is remarkable that today we have a world of information at the swipe of a finger and global positioning satellites orbiting overhead that tell us exactly where we are. There was a time, not so long ago, when a phone was just about summoning a voice on the other end of a line. But smart men and women in government, academia, and industry foresaw a world of a globally connected network of computers. In a few short decades, this audacious spirit has transformed all aspects of modern life, even if we now take it for granted.

It would behoove us to remember that America was conceived and built by risk-takers and explorers. We have been a land of movement, new thoughts, and unbridled audacity. One of the hallmarks of our national character is that we have, in the past at least, been quick to adapt to change. We have even thrived in eras of great transformation. For most of my lifetime, this has been a two-way conversation between government and society at large. We expected ourselves and those we elected to office to dream big and experiment, without fear of the failures that are invariably part of tackling tough challenges. This mindset led us to construct the Panama Canal; conquer the Great Depression; build highways, dams, and airports; create a social safety net; make progress on racial justice; lead a burgeoning scientific revolution; and so much more. Much of this was led by the government, no matter how unpopular that idea is with some politicians today. But there was a time when this role for government was considered a bipartisan mission.

It is true that big actions can also have big unintended consequences. The transcontinental railroad not only opened up the frontier, but it also sped the subjugation of the Native Americans and the exploitation of Chinese immigrant labor. Our highway system helped spur the primacy of the automobile, with its attending urban sprawl and pollution. The era of dam building provided water for us to drink and grow our crops, generated electricity, and protected against floods, but we now know that many dams also had severe environmental consequences. We cannot be afraid to act big, but we also cannot be afraid to reassess and address problems that may arise.

Unfortunately, in recent years, that can-do spirit has become nearly extinct in Washington, even as the engine of ingenuity burns bright in the entrepreneurial sectors of our citizenry. When did we accept a can't-do spirit from so many of our national leaders?

I am not sure when this erosion began. But these days the mission to the moon feels like more of a mission accomplished, if you're an optimist. A cynic might call it a dead end. Space may soon be a playground for the wealthy, but it is no longer a horizon of national importance. If you had told me that I would outlive the first great era of human space exploration, I never would have believed it. When the next era begins, and it most surely will, I'm not likely to be here to witness it. Will my children? Will my grandchildren?

When President John F. Kennedy came to Houston in September 1962 to issue a call to explore space, I was a young reporter excited to cover a big national story. I remember thinking that the real unknown was whether we could do it. I would never have thought to wonder whether we would care once we had. The Soviet Union was beating us in a great race for dominance, and in reality this was the biggest driver for our commitment. We as a nation felt vulnerable and lacking in self-confidence. But President Kennedy and his speechwriter Ted Sorensen crafted an inspirational call to action: The United States was going to the moon. And the president made it seem that all of us would be going along for the ride.

"But why, some say, the moon? Why choose this as our goal? . . . We choose to go to the moon in this decade and do the other things, not because they are easy, but because they are hard, because that goal will serve to organize and measure the best of our energies and skills, because that challenge is one that we are willing to accept, one we are unwilling to postpone, and one which we intend to win."

The president called it a choice, but it felt like a patriotic duty, full of optimism with a dash of dread at the thought that we might fail. For those of you who were not yet born, who did not live through it, this moment must now seem pregnant with portent in ways we could never have imagined. Who knew that this vibrant young president would be slain on a trip back to Texas a little more than a year later? Who could have imagined that after a handful of landings on the moon, no human from any country would thus far get close to doing it again? How naive would you have seemed if you said in September 1962 that the Cold War would be over in about thirty years without a single direct shot being fired between the United States and the Soviet Union?

Trying to summon that day in Houston, I keep returning to an image: The grass at Rice Stadium, the site of the speech, was damp. I remember it wasn't raining, and for years I thought perhaps it had been watered. But when I checked recently, I found out that the temperatures hit the nineties that day. And in Houston the heat dances with the devil of humidity. However, I don't remember it being hot. Perhaps that was because the president, well poised in his dark suit, seemed immune to it.

I was about to hear a speech calling for human beings to slip the bonds of Earth, and a shiver of remembrance shot through me. Five years earlier, I also had been standing on wet grass pondering the heavens. *Sputnik*, the first man-made satellite, had been launched by the Soviets in 1957. It was the shock to our national confidence that would culminate in Kennedy's speech and the race to the moon. But while *Sputnik* scared American policymakers, it awed me and many of my fellow countrymen. We were told that you could see it in the night sky as it passed overhead, a dot of light in orbit. One clear evening I headed out to search for it. As my bare feet stepped on the dew-dropped lawn of the house that Jean and I had just bought, I looked up and there it was.

Standing there at Rice Stadium, remembering *Sputnik*, I also thought of a far more distant moment, the first memory I have of my life. I was about four years old and in the yard at my maternal grandmother's house in Bloomington, Texas. "Put your hands in the dirt, Danny," I remember her saying. "Feel the richness of the dirt and then look to the stars." The dirt was indeed rich, and as I grasped at it, I remember looking up. The sky above was cloudless and twinkling, and it seemed unending. I was of this land, was the message from Grandma Paige. And yet I believe I sensed, even then, that there would be other horizons to ponder.

Audacity is not without risk, and exploration has always been about uncertainty as well as knowledge. It's about forging forward in the face of likely disappointment, even death. Kennedy knew this. He ended his speech with this exhortation: "As we set sail we ask God's blessing on the most hazardous and dangerous and greatest adventure on which man has ever embarked."

When we did land on the moon by the end of the 1960s, there was a sense that we were just beginning. A piloted mission to Mars was surely just around the corner. Boys across the country dreamed of being astronauts. (Sadly, at the time, it was a career goal that seemed implausible for girls.) Even I, into my fourth decade of life, hoped to travel into the great void—perhaps to be the first journalist in space. I feel a bit self-conscious to reveal now that I tried to keep myself in especially good physical shape in the late 1960s and 1970s, thinking, *Who knows? I might get the call to strap on a spacesuit.*

That, of course, didn't happen. And more broadly—and importantly—most of the predictions for piloted spaceflight never came true. The timeline for a trip to Mars still stretches onward with its own uncertain horizon. Our national will has changed. We seem to find money for tax cuts for the wealthy and foreign wars, but not enough for the exploration of space.

In the decades since the moon landing, the biggest stories around human spaceflight have been the tragedies, not the triumphs. In 1986 came the shock and catastrophe of the *Challenger* space shuttle explosion, which killed all seven crew members aboard, including schoolteacher Christa McAuliffe. Kennedy's warning that the journey into space would be "hazardous and dangerous" was tragically written against the blue sky in plumes of smoke and debris. As I sat at the anchor desk that day covering the breaking news, struggling, along with a shocked nation, to understand what had happened, I remember showing viewers the haunting pictures of the high school students in Concord, New Hampshire, who had gathered to see their teacher go into space. The memory still moves me.

A teacher heading into space had also inspired schools across the country to bring television sets into the classroom so that children could watch the *Challenger* launch live. And that night, when President Ronald Reagan addressed the nation, he had a special message for these young eyewitnesses to tragedy. "I know it is hard to understand, but sometimes painful things like this happen. It's all part of the process of exploration and discovery. It's all part of taking a chance and expanding man's horizons. The future doesn't belong to the fainthearted; it belongs to the brave. The *Challenger* crew was pulling us into the future, and we'll continue to follow them."

President Reagan promised to continue the "quest in space," and indeed, after a moratorium, the space shuttle program was renewed, but another tragedy would hit with the explosion of the *Columbia* space shuttle in 2003 and the deaths of seven more astronauts. Today we have largely retreated from piloted spaceflight, aside from the orbiting International Space Station. We understand that the difficulties of sending men and women to Mars have proven more substantial than we nonengineers might have thought all those years ago. And in the past few decades, unpiloted space exploration has led to far greater scientific discoveries than the *Apollo* mission ever produced. Even some scientists think that sending people into space isn't worth the cost and risk.

And yet the core of that speech by Kennedy in Houston was about something much bigger than debating a NASA budget or even space exploration. I keenly felt that day that we as citizens were being asked to embrace a larger purpose, one in which failure was not only an option but perhaps was also likely. The risk, however, was one we needed to take, together, as one nation—for ourselves, our species, and our planet Earth, with its wet grass underfoot. President Kennedy understood that there is something in the human character that can rally to big causes. A nation is strengthened when it can focus on a purpose. This impulse can be harnessed to ill effects, like wars of conquest. Or it can be used to turn unlikely dreams into reality.

At the same time the United States was closing in on the moon, the country embarked on a mission back on Earth that couldn't have been more different in spirit or objective. Whereas the space race was one of sharp national competition, this other effort would be deeply collaborative. The goal was to eradicate the deadliest killer known to man: smallpox. Like our voyages to the moon, this unprecedented public health mission was grounded in the audacious belief that our government could do something seemingly impossible, something that would change the course of human history.

In the twentieth century alone, an estimated three hundred million people had died of the disease, and we were determined to eliminate it entirely. The United States had been declared free of smallpox in 1949 after a major vaccination campaign. But the disease lingered, mostly in places we called the Third World at the time. The hope was that with proper determination and strategic deployments of public health workers, the entire world could be freed of a scourge that had been killing people by the millions since at least the time of the pharaohs in ancient Egypt. But there were many skeptics.

The effort was led by an unassuming epidemiologist from Ohio, D. A. Henderson (born just 150 or so miles away from a fellow Buckeye, Neil Armstrong). He had led a U.S.-sponsored vaccination program in West and Central Africa to great success. And many at the World Health Organization (WHO) took notice. There was a vote to see whether they should launch a global campaign, and the organization decided to do so by the slimmest of margins. The head of the WHO was livid, worried that the mission would be doomed to failure, much as what had happened with an earlier effort to eradicate malaria. So Dr. Henderson persuaded the United States to lead the effort to make sure his nation would feel responsible for success.

After a global campaign comprised of countless doctors, nurses, public health workers, and volunteers, smallpox was declared eradicated in 1980. It remains the only disease to have been fully defeated in the history of the planet. There is now hope that two more diseases could be added to the list: Guinea worm disease, whose eradication is being led by former president Jimmy Carter, and one of the plagues of my own childhood, polio.

The eradication of smallpox has been called the greatest medical event in human history. But the science behind it was relatively simple and well known. There had actually been a form of a smallpox vaccine since the eighteenth century; what was required was the ability to dream big, to work with others, and to see the destiny of the United States as improving the lives of those beyond our borders. This is the America of which I am exceptionally proud.

We see such ingenuity in America, from our great research universities to the proverbial garages of Silicon Valley, to all the decent men and women who go to work each day trying to make the country better as teachers, labor leaders, researchers, doctors and nurses, reporters, social workers, and so much more. We see incredible innovation in the private sector, but without governmental leadership, we are being held back. We do not need a heavy hand, just wise policies and an understanding that some things are so big or risky that only the government can be the catalyst for action.

One of the greatest challenges of our time is the need to generate abundant and nonpolluting energy. Early dreamers learned how to harness the wind to power their ships; later we learned the power of steam, and then fossil fuels. But today we see the dangers of our warming planet. Bold leadership could rally the nation to a revolution in clean energy. Already, governmental policies on energy efficiency and rebates for renewables have had a real effect. We need much more, but distressingly the current political tides seem to be carrying us in the opposite direction. I cannot fathom the shortsightedness of this policy. It should be clear to our political leaders that a new energy strategy could be the next technological revolution America could lead. But we are ceding the momentum to others such as China. Our planet and our national prosperity are already suffering from the decline in our leadership.

At a time when we desperately need to think boldly about the challenges before us, we find many of our politicians arguing that we need to be less ambitious. We hear from too many in Congress about why action is difficult, why something cannot be done. Many of our government agencies have now been turned over to people who are actively seeking to undermine the mission of those agencies. And our national needs go unaddressed. It is impossible to try to freeze ourselves in the status quo, and even more impossible to return to some mythic and misremembered glorious past. We need to remain a nation of new ideas and new initiatives, or we will cease to be the strong and daring country I know and love.

# Steady

I t was a winter night in late 1973 and, as was common during those days, I was coming home well after my children had gone to bed. My wife, Jean, was waiting for me at the small kitchen table in our town house in the Georgetown neighborhood of Washington, D.C. She'd set out a late dinner for me (to the best of my recollection, her famous Mexican salad). I sat down, and she sat down across from me. Looking me straight in the eye, she asked, "Are we going to be okay?"

It was a fair and honest question, and one for which I could not offer any of the assurances that I wished I had. She had heard the concern from neighbors and friends, whisperings that CBS News and, in particular, I, as the chief White House correspondent, were out on a limb on this Watergate story. "We have everything on the table," I said. I told her there was no place for us to run. "Either history is going to prove us right, or I will be looking for a new line of work."

This concern was not limited to the home front. The Washington bureau chief for CBS News, Bill Small, had alerted me that some very big names in the division, correspondents and executives, had come to him and said something to the effect of, "Rather may be a good reporter, but we think he bought a bad one here." I must stress that in the newsroom this was not the prevailing belief. My fellow White House correspondent Bob Pierpoint and I felt we had most of our colleagues' and superiors' support. And none more than Small himself. He was a rock of steadiness in our corner. As was the president of CBS News, Richard Salant. So we pressed forward.

But you couldn't be human and not worry. The *Washington Post* had led the story from the beginning, and we were following up. At least at first, there weren't many news organizations as invested as we were. I worried that the *New York Times*, which had excellent reporters, was being circumspect. What did they know that I didn't? It was pretty clear that the Nixon White House had a strategy of convincing the public that we were making far too much of a minor story. They tried to destabilize us. But in the end they failed, as they would eventually fail with the country at large.

At first, most of America wasn't paying very much attention to Watergate, but as developments began to tumble forth, the public became transfixed. What is so remarkable is how steady the nation remained during this constitutional crisis. In many other societies, a commander in chief so weakened would have destabilized the entire country, leading to riots, unrest in the streets, and maybe even the risk of a coup with tanks rolling down Pennsylvania Avenue. None of that happened, and I think most people were not surprised that our checks and balances remained resilient. I felt a supreme belief among the citizenry that we were a nation of laws and not of men. If President Richard Nixon had committed a crime, he would have to face the consequences, and our institutions of government would hold. We got refresher courses on the legal intricacies of impeachment, and when the end finally came, it was a remarkably peaceful transfer of power from President Nixon to President Gerald Ford.

The steadiness of the nation contrasted sharply with the increasing unsteadiness of President Nixon—the full measure of which we would not comprehend until after he'd left office. Later revelations would expose the frightening extent to which he was fueled by paranoia and lurched from rash decision to imprudent action. It was a stunning fall for an intelligent and accomplished politician, a former congressman, senator, and two-term vice president. Nixon, it turned out, had a fundamental unsteadiness in his character—a tragic flaw befitting a Shakespearean character that would ultimately prove his undoing.

When a nation sits atop the world order—and no nation in modern history has grown to become as powerful as the United States—that position comes with great responsibility. Yet danger lies where, as with Watergate, there is a reckless and impetuous hand at the helm. While we have a reputation as a young and sometimes brash republic, our greatest leaders have been men and women of prudence, wisdom, and composure. They have not been afraid to act boldly, but in most cases they have done so with discipline. They have been able to absorb shock and disappointment with resolution, steadfastness, and endurance. Our United States would never have survived against the incredible odds facing its birth and maturation without this sense of equilibrium, this steadiness.

As schoolchildren we learn of how George Washington held together his ragged army in the cold and forbidding Valley Forge on the road to independence. The grace and poise with which he established the precedents of the American presidency are equally remarkable. Without the brilliant determination of Abraham Lincoln, the Civil War, which cost hundreds of thousands of lives, could have ended the

American experiment forever. And while Dr. Martin Luther King Jr. is often remembered for his passion and the soaring rhetoric of his speeches, in covering him I was always struck by his calm and strategic mind as he carefully planned out his campaign for justice.

Don't get me wrong. Our nation must also embrace volatile voices. Some of our greatest artists and thinkers were men and women of turbulent and explosive minds and temperament. These are the cauldrons in which new ideas are formed. We need to be a society that hears the sometimes uncomfortable notes of radicalism. We need entrepreneurs who are willing to risk everything on wild dreams. But those risks must not be allowed to engulf the whole in chaos, especially in the governance of our country.

It will come as no surprise to those who have worked with me that one of my favorite words is "steady." It is the word I reached for when I had heard that President Kennedy had been shot. It was the word that I cautioned the world to heed after the terrorist attacks of September 11, 2001, as we were recoiling in a state of shock and horror. Many times I felt anxiety closing in, when my heartbeat quickened and my world began to wobble, and I repeated to myself, "Steady."

It is a word that I learned from my father, on account of its being one of his favorite words as well. When I was a child, I was stricken with rheumatic fever, and my parents feared that it would prove debilitating or even fatal. I was confined to my bed under doctor's orders and I have distinct memories of my mother weeping for my fate. She tried to cry as quietly as possible and out of earshot, but I heard her and it was frightening. The doctor suggested I keep my physical movement to a minimum, for fear that the disease would engulf my heart. It is difficult for a young boy to remain still in bed when the sun is shining and the world seems to be passing him by outside his bedroom window. I sometimes whimpered at the injustice of my fate, and my father would come into my room to stand over me, lovingly but firmly. "Steady, Danny," he would say. "Steady." The words were clear and deliberate, and they were soothing. At the time, I was too young to fully absorb his simple lesson.

To keep me occupied, my parents moved a radio into my bedroom, and it is there that I met my childhood hero, the great CBS News war reporter Edward R. Murrow. I listened to him for hours as he broadcast from London during the Blitz. These were very frightening times when it seemed that the world would succumb to the forces of evil. But the urgency of Murrow's voice, his signature opening—"This is London"—distracted my fevered mind and transported me from my small room in working-class Houston to the rooftops of Great Britain, where the stakes were bigger than my own. As the punishing sounds of a German aerial attack echoed in the background, Murrow described one of the most admirable features of the British character, the ability to stay steady. He told of thousands of people queuing up to enter the bomb shelters with order and a spirit of purpose. Murrow painted the picture with calmness and care. He was pretty darn steady himself.

I listened to Murrow and many others throughout the entire war, as I was slowed by another bout of rheumatic fever. In the early years of the war, the news was often grim. The dispatches were largely of setbacks, in Europe and then, after Pearl Harbor, in the Pacific. But slowly, the tides of war shifted. My lessons in world geography still consisted of obscure European towns and far-flung Pacific archipela-goes, but instead of datelines of Allied defeats, they became locations of stirring if bloody victories. I emerged from my illness with no long-term consequences to my health, and the United States emerged victorious at war. I had witnessed the great pendulum of personal and national fortune swing in the right direction, and I was armed with the lesson of my father, my hero Murrow, and my country: Stay "steady."

Even as I was growing up amid turmoil, I had a sense that a very different era had preceded my birth. The Roaring Twenties were related to me in stories that seemed to be of a distant time, although they were but a few years earlier. It was nicknamed the "decade of normalcy" and it had been anything but. It was a time of heady, giddy confidence. A Great War won (hailed at the time as the war to end all wars), and a stock market that only went up. And then it all crashed, leaving my parents and their generation knowing far too well the meaning of another important lesson in the human condition: the cost of arrogance.

Luckily the United States found itself under President Franklin Roosevelt, one of the most unwavering leaders in our history. In his first inaugural address, he exhorted his fellow citizens to respond to the despair of the Great Depression with steadiness and courage: "Let me assert my firm belief that the only thing we have to fear is . . . fear itself." But there is more to the quote. Roosevelt went on to link the action of that moment in history with the American tradition of resolve in the face of crisis. He called this fear "nameless, unreasoning, unjustified terror which paralyzes needed efforts to convert retreat into advance. In every dark hour of our national life a leadership of frankness and vigor has met with that understanding and support of the people themselves which is essential to victory." President Roosevelt's steadiness gave the nation the confidence it needed to overcome the twin challenges of economic hardship and war.

The very structure of our national government was conceived with steadiness in mind. Our Constitution was the product of the havoc that had beset the country under the weaker structure of the Articles of Confederation. But our founders, who had chafed under a monarchy, also worried about arrogance, and thus built a steady government with checks and balances on power to protect against malignant recklessness. Our House of Representatives—big, boisterous, and elected frequently—was set up to channel the changing passions of the populace, whereas the Senate was to be a place of deliberation. Our president was to be independently elected, but accountable to the other branches of government. An independent judiciary was to be able to rise above the pettiness of politics. Furthermore, through the federal system, the states would serve as their own "laboratories of democracy," to quote the great Supreme Court justice Louis Brandeis.

It has worked remarkably well, but we have sometimes, over the course of our history, lost our way into arrogance and unsteadiness. These are the flip sides of what is often referred to as American exceptionalism. It is true that we are a unique nation with a unique history. However, that does not bestow on us a birthright of superiority. When we have believed in our own invincibility, we have gotten into trouble.

I can vividly remember how, with the end of World War II, the national psyche of the United States brimmed with an unbridled confidence. Yes, the world was deeply damaged, the rise of communism loomed as an existential threat, and there were economic and social concerns here at home. But there was also a belief that the United States could solve any problem and conquer any challenge. In that confidence were the seeds of a looming conceit.

The Korean War, the war of my young adult life—called "the forgotten war" for a reason—is one to which we should all pay closer attention. Stuck between the glorious retellings of World War II and the contentious debate over Vietnam, the Korean conflict is often seen as tangential. I see it as transformative—for me personally, but also for the country because it changed the United States in fundamental ways.

Up until that point, when it came to war, America won. It always won (the Southern states in the Civil War being a notable exception). And why, at that time, would the country think otherwise? We had just fought a global two-ocean conflict and vanquished our enemies. In the years that followed, we continued to win everywhere—militarily, economically, socially, culturally. We were on a roll. Unstoppable. And then suddenly, seemingly out of nowhere, came the North Korean invasion. Our allies in South Korea were driven within a hairsbreadth of being pushed off the peninsula. And our armed forces were of little help at first.

No one had realized how hollowed out and unprepared our military was.

The myth of American invincibility after World War II had been pierced. And even though our military quickly reformed itself with the draft and a bold amphibious landing at Inchon, that decisive battle descended into a bloody slog of a war that ended in stalemate. It was a far cry from the clarifying conclusion to World War II. Furthermore, the battles in Korea were playing out against a larger backdrop of overconfidence. The American commander, the conquering hero of World War II Douglas MacArthur, had wanted to take the war to China, but President Harry Truman disagreed. Relying on the constitutional principle of civilian control of the armed forces, Truman fired MacArthur. It is an action that has been praised by historians and legal scholars, but at the time it did not play well with large swaths of the public. Meanwhile, back on the home front, much of the public was also convinced that the country was crawling with Americans spying for the Soviet Union. It was a time of the frenzied witch hunts of McCarthyism. The unity of purpose that had existed just a few years earlier had dissolved into recriminations and suspicion.

When the Korean War broke out, I was a student at the tiny Sam Houston State Teachers College, with a total enrollment of only about twenty-three hundred individuals. A large percentage of the male student body was either drafted or called up from the reserves, and I remember in particular a football teammate who left midseason. He returned, much faster than we expected, having been badly wounded. I was not eligible for the draft on account of my rheumatic fever as a child, but I felt the deep pull of a war that seemed to be my destiny to fight. It was how my friends felt as well. And I knew I was physically fit enough to serve, having started on my high school football team and even having had a brief stint on the squad in college. I was able-bodied and wanted to drop out of college to head to Asia to serve under the flag of my country. My mother would have none of it. Since I was the first in my family to attend college, she insisted, on familial pride, that a Rather would finish what he started.

I enrolled and trained in the Army Reserve while hurrying to finish college. I took summer classes to speed up my graduation and then enlisted in the U.S. Marines. After failing to truthfully answer a question about my childhood illness, I was sent to boot camp. I had the damn fool idea I was going to go in as the lowest enlisted man and rise to the rank of officer. I dreamed of a glorious military career. I reported for duty in San Diego with the full confidence and swagger of a former high school athlete. I wince now to think back at my exaggerated sense of self-worth on account of having graduated from college. At boot camp, I was destined to crash into a wall of reality. The goal of the drill sergeants in basic training was to tear us down and rebuild us in their image. They pushed me so hard physically that I suddenly became aware of my limitations. They also worked us over psychologically—"You are nothing," they would tell us. "You are insignificant" (although these sentiments were usually expressed in more colorful language).

This was all much more difficult than I'd imagined, but I was determined to show my mettle. And slowly, I began doing well. Then, for the first time in eight years, I started to get severe aches in my lower extremities. I was sent to the Marine doctors on base. As one examined me, he asked as a matter of course if I had ever had rheumatic fever. I said yes. The examination stopped instantly, and he looked at me and asked, quite pointedly, "You had rheumatic fever?" I knew better than to lie. "Yes, sir. I did." He walked away without uttering another word. I was pulled out of the ranks and sent to a "casual company"—"casual" being short for "casualty." I was forbidden to train. But the Marines being the Marines, no one sat around doing nothing. My job was to clean the noncommissioned officers' latrine—for days on end.

I didn't know it at the time, but the Marines had sent

a letter to my family doctor back in Houston, Louis Cope, asking about my medical record. He wrote back that I had indeed had rheumatic fever and he was appalled I had enlisted. I still have that letter. I was given a medical discharge, and one of the shortest and least distinguished careers in U.S. Marine history came to an end. I was humiliated and outraged. I knew I was fit to serve. I wanted to plead my case to the base commander. I got as far as an assistant who had no time or patience for my plight. I had never left Southern California. I would eventually see much war in my lifetime, far too much war. But I saw it carrying a reporter's notebook instead of a rifle.

So often when you feel most confident and most secure, you are in the greatest danger. After all, I had entered boot camp physically fit, having just graduated from college with good grades and a seemingly bright future. And I had found myself cleaning latrines. At the same time, my country, fresh off arguably the greatest military victory in history, was also bogged down in a land war in Asia and deep divisions at home. It was a kaleidoscope of events that was hard to handle and understand. I didn't have the perspective then, but now I can see that the Korean War was the start of a significant change in the way the country felt about itself.

We have never fully regained the confidence we felt at

the end of World War II, or the unity. Korea led to a long and arduous path of questioning our place in the world. We did not always win wars, as we would soon have to re-learn in Vietnam. We could not take our destiny for granted, as we began to realize under the shadow of the Cold War. There were deep ruptures and injustices within our nation, as we would see when the national spotlight shifted from the fissures of McCarthyism to the difficult struggle for civil rights.

Some may argue, and with merit, that ours is inherently a conservative system of government, one that has prevented rapid progress on a host of important issues. Unlike a parliamentary system, in which the leader of the executive branch derives his or her support from the legislature, we often have divided government with different political parties controlling the presidency and Congress. This can often stymie big actions. Whether one thinks that is a good thing or not, it usually depends on whether those in power align with your political views. When they do, we often chafe at their inability to get through their agenda. When they do not, we tend to revel in the checks on power within our system. An oppositional Democratic Congress stopped President George W. Bush from privatizing Social Security. And a Republican Congress stymied President Barack Obama's attempts to pass environmental legislation. How you respond to those two pieces of legislation depends more on your politics than your views on the separation of powers.

It is important to note that this stability of our system of government has only intermittently prevented progress. In the decades after the Korean War, we saw meaningful and positive action on racial and social justice, the economy and the environment, infrastructure, and workers' rights. But in recent years, I have worried increasingly that the mechanics of our government may be coming under a debilitating strain. We have seen two presidential elections in a short span where the winner of the popular vote did not win the antiquated electoral college. That is deeply troubling. Far greater political retrenchment, exacerbated by gerrymandered congressional districts, has led to political parties in Congress voting as blocs, with far less room for compromise. We have seen a push for far more ideological purity from our judges, and especially from those justices selected for the Supreme Court. We have seen inaction on important issues even where there is large agreement among the voting public—for example, on background checks for gun purchases, criminal justice reform, and campaign financing.

I see all this, and I am worried, but I hear the voice of my father once more: "Steady, Danny. Steady." I remind myself and others that we have been through big challenges in the past, that it often seems darkest in the present. The pendulum of our great nation seems to have swung toward conceit and unsteadiness once again, but it is in our power to wrest it back. Our government is there to serve us, not the other way around.

My friends, family, and colleagues will tell you that I have struggled, as most of us do, to walk the line between confidence and conceit. Such, I fear, is the human condition. It seems that each generation must in some way learn its own lessons about overreach. We would do well to study our history. For in it lies not only evidence of American greatness, but also the need for humility. And regardless of the invariable ups and downs that stretch before us in the future, I hope we can at least vow to try to remain steady. I would like to think that those around me would say that was one lesson I learned well.

One of the biggest tests to my own personal steadiness, and that of the nation, occurred with the assassination of President John F. Kennedy. In the chaotic hours after I had reported on his death from Dallas, I finally found a moment to call my wife, Jean, to see how she and our two young children were doing. She asked how I was holding up. I was somehow hanging in there, I said, and I could tell she was worried about me. I knew I had to get back to work, but this woman who understood me better than anyone else on earth had one final message to send me into the night. It has become one of my most cherished memories, and I have returned to it countless times for strength. "I love you," she said, and after a long pause, she added, "Steady."

# Courage

Manhattan is largely an island of straight lines—the avenues run north–south and the streets run east–west. Having lived in New York for much of my adult life, I have grown accustomed to charting my movements according to this urban grid. And for much of that time, I would undertake a daily western migration from my home on the East Side to the CBS Broadcast Center, which nearly abuts the Hudson River. This became a journey of such frequency that I knew all the landmarks on every possible route between the two points. I could catalog the colors of the awnings on the grand apartment buildings, and I could tell you which blocks were lined with the most trees. I would see the bustling bodegas and the queues of commuters awaiting the buses heading downtown. I witnessed the city as it oscillated between waves of confidence and doubt, triumph and tragedy. I saw businesses open and close, entire blocks demolished and replaced by shiny new construction. I often thought how, with all this change, the dreams of countless individuals were rising, and dying. It got to the point where I could predict the path of the sun in the sky for each season and the lengths of shadows it would cast amid the skyscrapers. Time ticked onward, years into decades, but I was so rooted in my routine that I felt it would go on forever, even though I knew, rationally, that all things must end.

And then, suddenly, it was all over. There would be no more journeys between those two points. A building I had entered almost as much as my own home was now off limits, and I knew I would probably never walk its hallways again. At first I was beset by anger—I felt I had been wronged, and I wanted answers. Few would come. The great wheel of fortune had spun, and this was where it had landed. With time, my anger began to recede, and it was replaced by a sense of emptiness and sadness. I bring this up not to revisit my departure from CBS News (plenty has already been written on that topic, probably too much, by me and by others), but to note that certainties can evaporate in an instant. A life path that you expected to stretch into the future can suddenly take you off a cliff. On the scale of human tragedy, this one was extremely minor. I, and my family, still had our health. I did not have to worry about my ability to put food on our table or a roof over our heads. I had already had a long and happy life. I knew how fortunate I was, and when I did sink into occasional periods of self-pity, Jean let me know in no uncertain terms how unattractive that quality was.

What I really didn't want to admit, least of all to myself, was that I was afraid. I was afraid that this was how it was going to end, that the final chapter of my professional career had been written. I was not really afraid about my public reputation. Sure, everyone wants to be liked, but I had long ago come to understand that being a reporter required you to raise unpleasant truths that would make you unpopular. As for whatever fame I had accrued over the course of my career, I can honestly say that I always saw that as fleeting. The news business is one mostly of the moment. But I still loved reporting and I didn't know if I was ever going to be able to do it again. Like an injured or aging slugger, I wondered whether I had rounded the bases for the last time.

All my adult life, I have prided myself on being a man who woke up each day and went to work. After I left CBS, I probably could have gotten a cushy emeritus position somewhere and ambled in and out of an office at times of my choosing. But those who knew me best understood, as I did, that this would have been a hollow and unfulfilling existence. My life had been dictated for years by a sense of order, in a career and a place of work. I could feel hints of chaos closing in.

When I would read the stories in the morning papers, I wanted to still be reporting myself. I was eager for meaningful work and, to be completely honest, to show that I still had it. Luckily, I got a chance with a weekly, one-hour cable news program called *Dan Rather Reports*. I assembled a team of top-notch reporters, producers, and editors, and it was pure joy. What we perhaps lacked in audience reach we more than made up for in editorial freedom. We traveled the world doing the type of deep-digging investigations and international reporting I have always cherished. We broke news and reported through long-form storytelling, the kind that had largely fallen out of favor at many network news divisions and cable channels.

I have long lived by the precept "Courage is being afraid, but going on anyhow." And eventually my fear of meaninglessness after CBS News dissipated. I felt I had not only persevered—I had thrived. Even after *Dan Rather Reports* ran its course, I was energized with a new sense of purpose. I embraced social media. I launched a production company, and I continue to read through several newspapers each morning looking for the next great story to chase.

My travels between work and home these days keep me mostly on the East Side of Manhattan. Occasionally, I have an event or a commitment that takes me west, and I find myself heading up Tenth Avenue past CBS News. I do not feel a tug in the chest or an overwhelming desire to turn my head. It would be nice to return at least once more to those halls that were home, but most of the people I knew there are gone. I can take memories of them with me wherever I go. Courage, I know, means going forward.

Recently, I have thought back to my own personal journey as the nation has careened into an existential crisis. The order of the past, of how governments were meant to run and how presidents were supposed to behave, has cracked. I worry especially for the young children. What must they think of our perilous state? My children and grandchildren are in adulthood, or approaching it. But I have heard from friends with children in grade school about the effects of this pervasive anxiety on young minds. One can only imagine the sense of disconnect that they feel. Children learn about our respected institutions of government and the steadfast leaders of our history in their textbooks, but the talk at home and on television describes an increasingly fragile system and increasingly vulnerable times.

I remember hearing from a scientist once that the

universe tends toward chaos, a sobering reality that underpins the laws that govern our planet and the vastness of space. But it is also a concept readily apparent to any of us who has tidied up a child's scattered toys or struggled to untangle a ball of string. It takes work to clean things up, to provide order. And these days, it feels as if our world is coming apart.

However, it would be fatalistic to think that we are powerless. Maybe we cannot change the equation at the level of the universe, but life is about creating order out of chaos. In the natural world, cells come together to form complex living beings. That's pretty orderly, and inspirational. And we can do something similar by bringing order to our own lives for the betterment of our community. The heroes we laud today in our history books are mostly men and women who stood up and said, "The work may be hard, the personal rewards uncertain, but we refuse to accept that the world cannot be made a better place."

The list of such people is long and wonderfully diverse. It includes women like Jane Addams, who pioneered social work, tended to the poor and the immigrant, advocated for women's rights, and won a Nobel Peace Prize. And it includes men like Jackie Robinson, who integrated Major League Baseball with courage and grace in the face of bigotry and hatred. There is Ida B. Wells, the African American investigative journalist and activist who exposed the horrors of lynching; John Muir, the naturalist and writer who helped convince America that its natural wonders should be protected; and Eleanor Roosevelt, who used her position of prominence to advocate for the marginalized and dispossessed. There is Harvey Milk, the first openly gay elected official in the United States, who was assassinated; Cesar Chavez, who fought on behalf of the rights of farmworkers; and "Fighting Bob" La Follette, the Republican governor and senator from Wisconsin who campaigned against political corruption and the corrosive effects of corporate power over our political system. These are but a few of the millions of Americans who, in ways big and small, famously and anonymously, have worked to make our nation more inclusive and just. When we think about a universe of chaos, it's helpful to remember Dr. Martin Luther King Jr.'s own equation for our journey through time and space: "The arc of the moral universe is long, but it bends toward justice."

This is a task that falls to each of us now, to summon the highest ideals of citizenship and patriotism and claim them as our birthright. Thirteen independent states joined, under an unprecedented national charter, to form the most improbable of unions. We have been tested many times. But thus far we have had leaders who have risen up to reaffirm that we have a common destiny. On March 4, 1865, with the bloody Civil War almost over, Abraham Lincoln was sworn in for his second term as president. His eyes were on the hard work of peace that would follow. "With malice toward none; with charity for all; with firmness in the right, as God gives us to see the right, let us strive on to finish the work we are in; to bind up the nation's wounds; to care for him who shall have borne the battle, and for his widow, and his orphan—to do all which may achieve and cherish a just, and a lasting peace, among ourselves, and with all nations." Lincoln understood that the United States had to be a land of compassion and empathy, but a lasting peace had to be a just one. A little over a month after he gave that stirring speech, he would be dead and the work of which he spoke far from finished. It always will be.

As we seek common ground with our fellow citizens, we cannot forsake our core values. Compromise cannot be confused with capitulation. Recently, many of you have come up to me and asked what can or should you do in a country you no longer seem to recognize. I have suggested, and will do so again here, that we all reach down deep into the soul of this nation and hold on to the central principles that have made us great. Do not let go. Do not apologize or explain away your brand of patriotism. Do not sacrifice your ideals.

Ultimately, democracy is an action more than a belief.

The people's voice, your voice, must be heard for it to have an effect. Currently, many hurdles diminish the power of our collective speech, such as how we finance campaigns, our discriminatory voting laws, and the preferred place of moneyed interests in Washington. Despite all these obstacles, I am enough of an optimist to believe that if we come together to speak, and vote, and participate, the nation will bend its path. It is especially important that we engage in action for our children. This struggle is not only about creating the country we wish them to inherit, it is also about teaching them (and relearning ourselves) how democracy is rooted in civic activity.

Holocaust survivor Elie Wiesel, in his acceptance speech for the Nobel Peace Prize, said, "I swore never to be silent whenever and wherever human beings endure suffering and humiliation. We must always take sides. Neutrality helps the oppressor, never the victim. Silence encourages the tormentor, never the tormented. Sometimes we must interfere." I am pleased that I had the opportunity to get to know Elie Wiesel, and that we became friends. I always stood in awe of his positive but determined approach to life, this from a man who had lost his parents and sister to the concentration camps. It is sometimes easy to magnify one's own struggles or the difficulties of the present age. In the face of people like Wiesel, or those who are confronting serious illness or economic hardship, I marvel anew at the resilience of the human spirit.

I understand that my time to shape and help this world is passing. This is the circle of life. I hope now to inspire others to love this country, to pledge to work hard to make it a healthier and more just place to live. I ultimately have faith in the basic decency of our American citizenry, and indeed people around the globe. I believe strongly that the core tenets I love most about this nation can be a foundation for commonality and strength once more. I believe in a wide and expansive vision of our national destiny. And I believe in all of you to help make it a reality. Courage.

# Acknowledgments

This book is a product of more than eight decades of living and loving my country, but it would not have been possible without the last several satisfying and encouraging years of my career—ones for which I am extremely appreciative. I have long said that I am a reporter who got lucky, very lucky. This luck began early, with wonderful family, friends, teachers, and mentors. And it has remarkably continued into the present, an unlikely and unexpected chapter of my life.

For this I will always owe a debt of gratitude to Mark Cuban, who allowed me to continue with my lifelong love of journalism. Many of the ideas for this book grew out of the years at *Dan Rather Reports*, which Mark made possible with his financial and moral support. He is a firm believer that this country benefits from a vibrant and fearless press and that the necessary debates of governance are useless without an informed citizenry.

I would like to thank the wonderful, intelligent, and dedicated staff at *Dan Rather Reports*. I consider what we produced some of the best work of my career. Away from the trappings of network news, I reconnected with my country and its people in simple but powerful ways that reaffirmed my belief in the basic dignity and honesty of my fellow citizens. Being around young, energetic journalists filled me with optimism for the future of our country that I hope is evident in this book. I see new generations of clear-eyed patriots who love America enough to want to make it a better place.

*Dan Rather Reports* was led by executive producer Wayne Nelson, a fellow Texan and pure newsman. Wayne is indefatigable in chasing down a story and making sure the reporting is fair and true. His broad interests led us to report on wide-ranging stories, which helped provide a foundation for many essays in the book. He is now ensuring that the highest traditions in journalism are a cornerstone of my production company, News and Guts. My hope is that we can pursue production projects that build off the themes of this book, and I am thankful for having my longtime colleague Phil Kim lead the development of these efforts. He is a trusted visionary who understands that in a changing media world, we cannot be afraid to adapt and experiment while holding true to our ideals.

Much of the spirit for *What Unites Us* came out of my surprising experience on social media. It was a strategy conceived and implemented by my coauthor, Elliot Kirschner (who was also the senior producer on *Dan Rather Reports*). As we collaborated on tone, style, and writing, he proposed we do the kinds of posts we wanted, and not worry if they were too long or too nuanced for the conventional wisdoms of Facebook. He was right, and I am grateful.

Thanks to our Facebook profile, we came to the attention of Kathy Pories, an editor at Algonquin Books. She reached out, and this book idea was born. Kathy doesn't only deserve credit for the inception of this project; she has served as the book's incomparable editor. With high standards and a clarity of perspective, she has prompted and polished these essays into their final form. Betsy Gleick, the editorial director at Algonquin, has been an enthusiastic and encouraging supporter of this project since the beginning. Her confidence that this was a book worth writing, and that its messages were urgent and timely, sustained us. And I know that publishing a book takes a broad and diverse team working behind the scenes, so a big thank-you to everyone at Algonquin who made this happen.

I couldn't do what I do without the invaluable help of Alex Van Amson, who keeps me informed, on track, and on time, as best she can. I also am grateful for Felicity Thompson's detailed fact-checking on this book.

And, as always and forever, my appreciation and love to fighting heart Jean Grace Goebel Rather, my wife, lifelong supporter, and major contributor to this book.

Finally, I would like to give a tip of the Stetson to all of you. I believe deeply that this nation will thrive, not only because of its institutions but also because of its people. One of the great joys of these recent years on social media has been to read your many thoughtful comments. Seeing my fellow citizens and people from other countries eloquently and passionately sharing their hopes, fears, and dreams for the future of the United States and its place in the world fills me with optimism. My greatest desire for this book is that it encourage conversation and debate about what it means to be an American today, and more broadly over the course of this nation's history. If we stand firm in our better values, do not shy away from challenging injustice, and can talk to one another rather than past one another, I am confident we can find the common ground that unites us.